COMPASS
of the
HEART

COMPASS

of the

HEART

embodying

medicine

wheel

teachings

LOREN CRUDEN

Destiny Books
Rochester, Vermont

Destiny Books
One Park Street
Rochester, Vermont 05767

LIBRARY OF CONGRESS CATALOGING-IN-PUBLICATION DATA
Cruden, Loren, 1952–
    Compass of the heart : embodying medicine wheel teachings / Loren Cruden.
    p. cm.
    ISBN 0-89281-600-7 (pbk.)
    1. Shamanism—North America. 2. Medicine wheels. 3. Spiritual life. 4. Spiritual exercises. I. Title
BF1622.U6C78 1996
299'.93—dc20   95-48807
                                                               CIP

Printed and bound Canada

10 9 8 7 6 5 4 3 2 1

Text design by Tim Jones

Text layout by Virginia L. Scott

This book was typeset in Janson text with Berliner Grotesque as the display typeface

Destiny Books is a division of Inner Traditions International

Distributed to the book trade in Canada by Publishers Group West (PGW), Toronto, Ontario

Distributed to the book trade in the United Kingdom by Deep Books, London

Distributed to the book trade in Australia by Millennium Books, Newtown, N. S. W.

Distributed to the book trade in New Zealand by Tandem Press, Auckland

Distributed to the book trade in South Africa by Alternative Books, Randburg

*To my land partner
and friend,
Robin Gillis*

CONTENTS

Part Three: West—Water

Part Four: North—Stone

Part Five: Earth

Part Six: Sky

Part Seven: Center

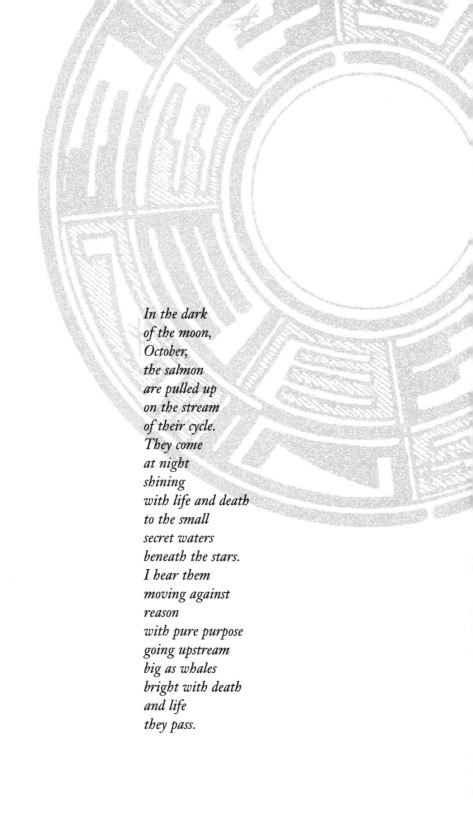

In the dark
of the moon,
October,
the salmon
are pulled up
on the stream
of their cycle.
They come
at night
shining
with life and death
to the small
secret waters
beneath the stars.
I hear them
moving against
reason
with pure purpose
going upstream
big as whales
bright with death
and life
they pass.

Introduction
THE JOURNEY HOMEWARD

The path of consciousness for Earthly beings is an unfoldment of embodied spirit. If you think of consciousness as something you participate in rather than something you have, your orientation shifts; such a pervasive sense of consciousness allows you to see your spiritual nature. Consciousness expresses—embodies—itself in forms that range from the most etheric to the most substantial. Life's web is a complexity of those manifestations: spruce tree, rainbow, bat, lava, human being—each carries the light of common cosmic origin, the potential within the Mind of the Mystery. Awakening to Spirit's presence through the experience of embodiment and its moment-to-moment opportunities for connection within the web of life gives impetus and direction to homeward yearning. This is the process of Self-knowing.

Within this process, the usefulness of following a prescribed spiritual path is its focus of awareness. Every path has its inherent strengths and weaknesses, though the strengths are often not perceived by the doubtful and the weaknesses unacknowledged by the zealous. An imposition of dogma tends to devitalize a path's strengths, turning it into a spiritual treadmill. However, despite pitfalls, teachings along a given path can be keys to transcendent consciousness. The important consideration is this: Whether the path involves yoga, Christian mysticism, Zen Buddhism, shamanism, or some nameless singular or eclectic exploration into the nature of Being, for it to be nourishing it must taste of home. Like a salmon moving out of the vast communal sea into a particular river leading to a certain creek, each individual must find the stream of truth that sings of home.

A path itself provides access, a way to journey, but for realization to unfold there must be movement, action kindled by the heart's desire. Daily spiritual practices are steps that help guide choice and action by facilitating alignment with Spirit. They give orientation and positive channel for life's flow.

The practices may include such various things as meditation, work with chakras, teaching children, gardening, prayer, martial arts, or smiling at strangers—any daily actions thoughtfully made can be considered spiritual practice. The importance is awakened, spirit-aligned movement, not investment in philosophic disciplines. There should be joy in these practices—aliveness, transformation, expansion, revelation, beauty. Daily practices are ways of maintaining connectedness to truth through the ups and downs of experience. They enhance awareness and perspective. The prayer at dawn is a reminder of spiritual reality: Yes, life is a sacred gift. I am alive in this opportune moment, breathing, in gratitude for the light of this new day.

These practices widen a path's access until gradually spiritual awareness is not an intermittent inspiration but is life itself. Each thought, action, and experience is a holographic part of this spiritual reality. The enlightened dawn becomes the enlightened life. The path becomes the universe, the practice each breath. At first practices create the way; later they simply express the way.

Path and practice, in their many guises, are two aspects of embodied spirituality. A third aspect is participation. Regardless of how personal the path; regardless of how ordinary or esoteric the practices, the reality of consciousness is that it is pervasive, not just disparate. Participation is how you honor that reality. The individual dance is inseparable from cosmic destiny. Each individual's participation can be guided by a perspective of wholeness.

Participation is commitment to being fully present in life. It is living in the same manner as the salmon—leaping up the waterfall, not holding back. The bear's smashing paw, the eagle's snatching talons, the rock's jagged edge, the fisherman's eager net do not discourage the salmon from its shimmering leap. Commitment is unconditionally acted upon again and again. The salmon does not seek bargains or bemoan its circumstances. There are no failures in this participation no matter the outcome. The successful return to the spawning grounds perpetuates a cycle of renewal. The bear's paw can be a gateway of transformation also, serving life's continuity.

Often in moving on a spiritual path obstacles arise, seemingly becoming larger and more frequent the further you travel. Spiritual maturation is not an absence of difficulties. It is a deepening of equanimity that uses difficulty to guide awareness to what needs attention or healing. In Buddhism this is called "practicing against the grain." It is the salmon's upstream journey washing away hindrances in thought, emotion, and habit. Movement through this current strengthens awareness and capacity. The surrender to going upstream embraces that which sweeps away doubt and halfheartedness. The current calls you to fully engage, awaken all your abilities, connect with your deepest resource and belief. This is the practice that determinedly faces fear, confusion, sloppiness of mind, pretension, and procrastination. In the upper reaches of their journey, the salmon often have to wriggle over branches, squirm between rocks, and patiently find an ever more singular path homeward.

This book is dedicated to those who are making the salmon's journey: the journey of openhearted participation that gives priority to wholly seeing, knowing, and moving in a stream of truth; the practice that leaps homeward again in spite of all—because of all—because of love. It is love that guides the compass of the heart. Love helps you recognize Spirit in life and gives courage for your participation.

The teachings given here arose naturally during the cycles of life. The stream of truth that sings to me is one of beauty—at once ancient and ever new. When I write I often sit in a rocking chair looking out on the mountain that is my home. I rock and gaze, listening to the mountain, watching a hunting hawk or a browsing deer or a caravan of clouds. With no phone or electricity, the house is still—my son away at college, cats curled on the bed, towns and roads miles away.

Trees gaze back: firs, aspens, larches, cedars. In summer a hummingbird may zoom close, piercing my faraway focus with its needle beak and buzzing wings, then zoom away again. I write these words from a stillness touched by bird, by cloud, by tree, by mountain. As other human beings negotiate traffic, or stride corporate corridors, or shield their faces from the sear of smelting furnaces, or shamanize in the cities, I keep this particular continuity—being a human who lives intimately with the natural Earth.

When I go to the city to teach, people express a need to reconnect with a clarity of life within Life. Modern Western perspective is conditioned to a view that identifies self with ego; spirituality is difficult to experience within such confines. An expanded perspective provides a view wherein the ego is not the center of the universe. Within this perspective, spirituality becomes the context, not an adjunct or accessory to being.

The vision quester coming to the mountain asks "How do I participate?" as he gives his offering to the fire. My book *The Spirit of Place* (1995) presented some practices for integrating body and spirit, in order to reconnect with an expanded experience of being. *Compass of the Heart* offers perspectives for practitioners—those who are presently living a life dedicated to sacred alignment and want to open to further possibilities.

This book is about natural spirituality, not religion or a particular program of practice. Natural spirituality is the birthright of a consciousness embodied in Earthly life, and it honors the gifts of that life. I think of natural spirituality as the integration of body (earth) and spirit, an organic enactment of connectedness to Source. Its orientation is to right relationship with all. With its spectrum of manifested forms, life gives you the opportunity for constant feedback. In a web of kinship—through interactions with the land, its creatures, the elements, and your own species—you learn about relationship. You can find an expansion of self in the many facets of consciousness that emanate from the center of Being. You find that Self has a spaciousness without edges.

This is natural spirituality: a compassionate and manifested awareness of inherent connectedness to all. It is spirituality that belongs to no particular gender, race, age, system, or path. Its only prerequisites are awareness and respectful participation. All else unfolds from these.

Unlike the practices described in *The Spirit of Place*, which are appropriate for practitioners of all levels, some of what is presented here is not a precinct for those without preliminary training or development of capacity. Lacking a strong foundation for application, it can be frustrating, confusing, or even dangerous to engage in practices for which there is not adequate preparation or support. This refers especially to such things as conducting sweat lodges or guiding people on vision quests. These are life-altering ceremonial forms whose outward appearances are deceptively simple.

The Spirit of Place emphasized orientation and practice within an expanded, integrated perspective of self. This book assumes access to and ongoing movement within the realm of Spirit. Focus is now directed to clarity of participation. In writing this book I saw two possible roads: one of presenting "advanced" techniques and the other of moving deeper into understanding the core of spirituality. The choice for the book was the same as for my life—the path of primality. Techniques are directionless without grounding and connection to Source; they are style without substance. If you are working with a traditional path, techniques can be learned from teachers aligned with that path. If you are creating a more singular journey, tools will organically evolve over time.

What are shared in this text are insights, suggestions, and mirrors of experience that will perhaps resonate with or awaken an aspect of the practitioner's own truth, thus initiating movement. Those "Aha!" moments of resonance may catalyze leaps of awareness that bridge what before were isolated concepts or dormant, unarticulated perceptions. When spiritual inquiry blossoms beyond the closed circle of intellectual debate and self-absorption, true unfolding is possible.

Understanding, applied to daily life, opens the way for change.

I sit writing this in the light of a spring evening, pondering the inner landscape as I gaze past the glass doors of my mountain home. Abruptly (but absently) I notice a large animal muzzle nosing the ground inches from the glass. Concentration still turned inward, I am marginally aware that my cats are behaving oddly, tiptoeing to the window—avoiding the glass doors—and peering excitedly out. Focus becoming more present, I see the dog asleep on the rug, and understanding dawns that she therefore cannot be the animal attached to the snout outside. As this realization penetrates and the animal moves into full view, I am at last cognizant of the fact that there is a bear snuffling around a slight distance from where I sit. My oblivion has been hardly less profound than the dog's slumber.

Heart now pounding, I join the cats in watching the bear. We are torn between silent fascination and the urge to assert our territorial perogative. The bear soon loses interest in the patio stones and ambles off to investigate the compost bin, then disappears into the forest.

The metaphor that occurs to me as I return (with some residual agitation) to my writing has to do with the hope that something in this book will perhaps joggle your preoccupations or interupt your immersion in knowledge, awakening an immediacy of what you are and what you are doing. It is my hope that this book be sort of a heyoka bear on your doorstep; not something looking for a following or claiming to have answers, but something snuffling around in the extraordinary fullness and potential of the present moment.

The text of this book is arranged in the form of a medicine wheel, a natural mandala of experience. It may be useful to work with *The Spirit of Place* first as an introduction to what is presented here, but each book stands on its own. In both, I have tried to write certainly not all there is to say on each topic addressed, but things I have not seen elsewhere. Rather than exhaustive coverage I have tried to alight on aspects that seem particularly applicable to the concerns and needs of people in these times. No matter what you perceive your path to be or what practices you choose in support of it; no matter if you perceive no path at all and your practices are spontaneous expressions of spiritual inspiration, the compass of the heart is what guides the journey homeward.

This precious life is not a time for allowing fear to hold us back. Unlike the salmon we have built the dams that obstruct our rightful journeys, and we have the tools with which to clear the way. May we use them for the freedom of all.

Altar of wind—
vision carried
leaflike to speak
in sympathy to
other lands.
Winds of dawn
bringing the light
into remembrance
gold upon the rocks
reflected and held
in solitude unmined.
Night winds,
the thoughts of
conjurers, owl wings
on the fingertips
of consciousness,
prayers sent
with fragrance of wild roses—
altar of wind.

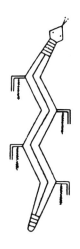

PART ONE

East
Wind

one

THE MEDICINE WHEEL

In 1981, when I began to work with Lewis Sawaquat, a Native medicine man, one of the first (and few) things he asked me to do was to offer a prayer to the cardinal directions every morning and every evening. He did not say what to associate with those directions, he just suggested I pray and pay attention. In this way I approached the medicine wheel.

There is no one traditional medicine wheel, nor is there any consensus about what *medicine wheel* refers to. Like *medicine*, it is a term whose invention may be modern but whose meaning is ancient and global. Certainly many tribes do not use a circle of stones to describe their relationship with the Six Powers (the four Cardinal Directions, Earth, and Sky), although most land-based spiritual paths—whether of Native American, European, or other origin—have oriented spiritually to these directional powers. A medicine wheel is one way of naming and using that orientation.

Interaction with a medicine wheel offers many layers of understanding. The wheel is a map of life, and just as you can name, explore, and understand life from many different perspectives, you can work with a medicine wheel from a multitude of approaches, each one adding dimensions of experience and realization.

Use of the wheel is sometimes ceremonial, and therefore external, but always there is an echoing back and forth through the realms of consciousness that makes the physical aspect of ceremony more than it appears. The integration of medicine-wheel consciousness into daily awareness brings medicine-wheel teachings and power into the moments beyond ceremonial occasion. When this happens, the wheel is more deeply experienced as a mandala that can guide ordinary outlook into sacred awakening. This multileveled application will be focused on throughout this book.

The correspondences that I use in exploring the medicine wheel are not particular to any established tradition and are no more valid than any other. What I use comes from my own evolution in this work. It is shared here as an example, not as the one true way or as an explanation of Native American philosophy.

Let us move in this exploration as in a ceremony. We enter this wheel in the East. Here the sun rises, life awakens, intelligence is quickened. Here we choose a focus for awareness and action: intention is conceived.

Air is the element of the East. This is the realm of breath, of thought, of sight, of communication. The medicine pipe is here in its association with truth-speaking and sacred use of the breath.

Seekers rise at dawn to meditate or pray, to use the mind and breath in alignment with Spirit. East is the precinct of concentration and recognition. It is where desire focuses on a course of manifestation. East is the spring-planted seed that will come to fruition in accordance with its nature.

Wolf is here as pathfinder and teacher of keen sense and applied intelligence. Eagle is here—giver of wide, accurate perspective and ethical courage. Tobacco is here too; as we stand in the East we fill the medicine pipe with tobacco that carries our prayers, our intentions, and our understandings of truth.

We move now to the South. As awareness is the power of the East, alignment is the medicine of the South. The sun is at midheaven here—there is no shadow. South's teaching is of action within right relationship. It is connectedness and touching. It is making alliance with your relations. Vision-questing is here, the seeking of spiritual destiny and the guides who will help us on the path. Sundance is here—the committed personal participation in what is good for all.

Fire is the element of the South: friction, energy in transformative movement, sexuality's creative and ecstatic flame. Desire's intention—energy of the East—seeks affirmation in the integrity of life's resources in the South. Coyote is here—creator and fool, medicine of mirroring, teacher about ego in this place of relationship.

Sit by the fire and regard your East-conceived intentions in the light of right kinship. Who are your allies here and what is your dance in this life?

The way leads West now, place of the setting sun, the twilight. We stand on the other side of day: a realm of reflection, introspection, and the unknown. The outward-looking East is balanced by inward awareness in the West. It is a place of listening, of altered states, of fluid consciousness. The listening serves acceptance and thus growth.

The twilight is a betweenness that gives access to subtle worlds. Here we discover if we have heart for the work of Spirit: the path of maturation; the release of limiting beliefs about self and reality; the putting aside of personal likes, dislikes, judgments, and opinions that obscure wholeheartedness and transcendence.

West is the drum's transporting pulse, the power of ceremony and dream, the place where beliefs are dismantled and boundaries dissolved. The mysterious and awesome Thunderbeings are here with their inexplicable agendas. Bear is here—dream medicine, companion on the healing path.

In the West, the clarity and alignment of intention we carry from the East and South is swirled through the many realms of consciousness like a leaf in a series of whirlpools. It is assailed by self-doubt, denial, and confusion. Desire becomes awash in emotion. From the depths of the West's listening comes stillness. The autumn tree lets go its leaves and does not die, does not lose its truth of Being. This is the teaching of the West.

From here we move North. It is night. Groundedness is what guides us here—our feet know the way. It is not appearance that we trust now, it is the wisdom of a rooted alignment. All else is change—cycles and transformations spiral us deeper into integration.

North is the actualization of intention. It is where the seeds planted in the East bear their first fruit. Earth is the element here; it is through embodiment of sacred desire that we fulfill our Earthly journeys. North is where Spirit is manifested in a completion of growth and enactment. Here we find community and our service in the web of relationship. Here we learn to prioritize our efforts in accordance with harmonious participation.

Buffalo is present, teacher of the giveaway and of the abundance this allows for all. Quartz is here, showing us how to amplify, house, or transmit energy and knowledge. North is the home of the sweat lodge—the purification, the elemental arena of encounter, meeting place of all worlds.

Stand in the North, in the starry winter night, and commune with your ancestors, knowing someday your feet too will walk that path to the Milky Way. Know this and tend to your work upon this Earth.

Is the journey finished? No, the wheel moves us again to the East, to begin anew. Face the gate of morning and light the pipe you filled so long ago. Smoke these prayers that have moved with us—intentions that were conceived, aligned, accepted, and actualized. Smoke the truth that is in them and give the ashes to the wind. It is a new day.

The perimeter of the wheel is only one of its paths, and includes the directional stations and the movements between them. A wheel's cross-quarters, sometimes referred to as its "winds," are all directions integrating the qualities of the cardinal points they fall between. Cross-quarter medicine work often relates to change, healing, and the dislodgment of fixed perspectives. Sometimes a wheel's perimeter is arranged with three stations between each two directions, the intermediate stations representing the months or "moons" of the year. The perimeter can be subdivided endlessly into smaller and smaller degrees, using traditional or personally devised systems or designations. Each subdivision is a station in its own right.

But the wheel is not just a circle. Because it is a map of the universe, it is multidimensional. Above is the Sky. This is where expansion, extended vision, destiny, and possibility open before you. Below is the Earth—the sacred ground, teacher of timing, providence, orientation, nourishment, and commitment. As an embodied spirit you bridge these realms, experiencing the gifts of both.

Crossing the circle are the East–West and South–North roads, which meet and intersect in the wheel's center. Extend your wheel exploration to include these two paths. Turn from your position in the East to face the West. The East–West road lies before you, sunrise to sunset to sunrise. It is a path of cycles—rising and setting, breathing in and breathing out, sowing and reaping, focus and release, hope and acceptance. The East–West road is where you do your self-analysis, understanding, patterning and unpatterning, structuring and destructuring, looking out and looking in.

Natives call this road the Black Road. It is a path heavily trodden by modern people. Like all aspects of the medicine wheel, there is no lesser value to it as long as it does not become the only path used. Work with the East–West road needs to be part of a larger experience and perspective.

In the East you use your mind to focus, conceptualize, and understand. You sharpen your awareness through disciplines of meditation, visualization, concentration, and attention. East is where things dawn on you, awaken in you, spring into being. In its light you find illumination and insight; things are recognized and become known. You are inspired and formulate intention.

Concepts become beliefs, structures of your personal paradigm. You identify with them and they become your outlook on life, on self. As you travel the East–West road you encounter powerful waters, emotions and states of consciousness that shake and dissolve beliefs. Outlook turns inward. If the mirror of self found there is not still and clear, the reflection is distorted. What is seen within this rippled surface can bring reactions of fear, constriction, and doubt.

West, the realm of emotion, is fluid, and undermines the East's certainty. The East–West dance can be a classic struggle between objective and subjective aspects of consciousness. This struggle only exists by virtue of believing that these aspects are separate. On the East–West path you tend to teeter from one end to the other.

Integration can only be realized from the center.

In the West beliefs are dismantled, their energies released or rearranged. This can happen deliberately through altered states of consciousness—dreams and trance, for example—or haphazardly through such things as drug use, emotional intensities, and trauma. West's twilight is where what was recognizable in the light of dawn loses its definition in the strange dimness of evening. If you perceive through the distortion of fear, what is then carried back into the East's realm of conceptualization are beliefs shaped and charged by that fear. If acceptance and love clear your gaze instead, what is seen and translated into belief are realizations that bring greater freedom and healing.

The East's disciplines of the mind develop focused awareness and conscious intention. The West's work with emotions develops expanded access to transformational states—the capacity to open and change. Understanding the dynamics and possibilities of this path is essential to understanding medicine work. The formation and transcendence of beliefs and the use of altered states to destructure and rearrange patterns within a sacred context is the basis for most healing. Psychology sometimes makes a rough attempt at traveling this path. Therapists who utilize spiritual approaches in the context of their work begin to connect with the potentials of the East–West road.

The East–West axis is the interplay of thought and emotion, mind and heart, perception and intuition. It is the path of Being, the path on which we learn about consciousness.

The South–North road, balanced between belief and non-belief, is what Natives call the Red Road. It is the path of doing. On this path you listen to the voices of both the right and left hemispheres of the brain, to both heart and mind, and to the needs to be both sure and uncertain, dutiful and spontaneous, guided and free.

South is where individuality is mirrored and expressed. It is the vigorous realm of reaching, comparing, contrasting, exploring, experimenting, encountering. It is relationship's precinct. Here soul takes on personality and feels its uniqueness. In a pure sense soul becomes ego—a particular manifestation of wholeness. Here it experiences union through the channels of alliance and sexuality: the One becoming many, the many becoming One. The teachings of ego are here—bravery, honor, self-respect, confidence, passion—and also the pitfalls of egotism—conceit, greed, vanity, selfishness, malice.

As self experiences self through the mirrors of relationship, identity expands into interconnectedness and interdependency, the northward path. North is where community abides as a fully woven tapestry of manifested spirit. The South–North road is the maturation of individualized experience into actualized wholeness. The unique solos, duets, quartets, and other arrangements of the South are brought into harmony with the North's vast orchestra. On this path you learn to integrate self-nurturance with generosity toward others; you learn how nourishment is shared and abundance thereby increased through the non-grasping realization of wholeness.

North is manifestation—walking your talk. It is where healing reaches physical dimensions. It is where you gain the mountain's summit and realize that you must climb down again; you realize that life is not linear, that there is no ending. You cannot cling to knowledge, to accomplishment, to status, to complacent systems. On the South–North axis the rocklike fixity of the North is balanced by the dancing volatility of the South's fire, as the surety of the East is kept on its toes by the unknown depths of the West.

The South–North path is an unfolding of Life's desire to express itself in a multiplicity of fulfillment, of form. It is spirit in body, the enactment of sacred relationship on a material plane. Here you learn to apply your gifts in the world. The vision-quester takes what has been revealed in his solitude back to the tribe. This is the essence of the South–North path. Those oriented to the East–West road would try to find how to fit the vision into their lives; on the South–North road, life is aligned with the vision. An East–West practitioner uses spirituality for personal growth. A South–North practitioner uses personal growth for Spirit. Old time medicine people tended to walk the South–North path, applying insight and power directly to the needs of the tribe. New Agers tend to work the East–West road. It is a shift of the times and of culture. It is hard to imagine Natives of the past having an existential crisis on the buffalo hunt or being preoccupied with analyzing dysfunctional family patterns.

The exploration of these two roads on the medicine wheel eventually brings the seeker to the center. It is here that I think the old time medicine and the modern approaches will find their completion in consciousness and in the world. The center is where all roads meet and balance. It is where all directions have their origins and all truth has its essential alignment. From the center you have access to all perspectives and resources. Here being and doing are joined, each equally predicated on the other. The center is not a static place—it is where movement in and experience of all realms, all aspects of reality, are simultaneously available. It is here that the portal of the wheel opens to absolute freedom of consciousness, the Mystery's doorstep.

two

BREATH

When East is regarded as the realm of air, perception becomes directly linked not only to thought, awareness, and brain function, but also to breath. And when life is regarded as sacred, the breath is naturally central to the experience of sacredness. Whether used as the focus of meditative concentration, or for hymn singing, prayer, recitation of mantras, invocation, Tantric practices, trance access, holotropic release, New Age affirmations, yoga, chakra clearing, or channeling force in martial arts, the breath is the vehicle for present-moment attention and movement of intention and energy.

The breath has four aspects: the inhalation, the exhalation, and the pauses between. The inbreath is an expression of hope and participation. It takes in; it is communal; it says "Yes" to being on Earth, to being alive. It embraces the new moment and believes in continuity. Though it may be shallow or tentative, robust or ecstatic, always the inbreath is an agreement to be here.

The outbreath is a manifestation of trust. It is a letting go that allows the next gift to be received. The more complete the out-breath—the deeper the relaxation and trust—the more space there is for the inbreath that follows. The outbreath gives testimony to the balance of cycles and the necessity of movement in order for life to exist and flourish.

The pause between outbreath and inbreath is a stillpoint where consciousness can drift past boundaries. It is in this stillpoint that consciousness leaves the body in death, and can enact temporary departures during trance. It is in this pause that choices are made about the next breath. The stillpoint is a gate with many options. Long pauses between outbreath and inbreath can demonstrate ambiguity or a tendency for consciousness to journey.

The pause between inbreath and outbreath is a moment for savoring life and abiding in fullness, poised for action. It can be an expression of awe and appreciation. As part of the natural cycle of breathing, the pause brings alertness and presence. In some esoteric practices the breath is held—this pause intentionally sustained—in order to consolidate energies. This is different from breath-holding that is an unconscious fear response when one feels threatened.

Attention to the balances and rhythms of these aspects of breathing brings insight and the awareness of ever-present avenues for change. Ancient teachings, such as those of pranayama, focus on the breath. There are also some modern therapies that use modified versions of old practices. Some contemporary breathwork therapies emphasize and encourage emotional catharsis or heightened states of awareness brought on by hyperventilating or otherwise manipulating oxygen flow; such practices can create panic conditions in the body that encourage emotions or traumas to surface. These experiences are oftentimes confused with shamanic or transcendent states of consciousness because of the vivid imagery, amplified feelings, and extraordinary sensations that usually accompany them.

More mundane but no less important are cathartic releases through exaggerated breathing that come through laughter or sobbing. Any time the breath forcefully accelerates, there is an emotional urgency that concurrently arises. If release is achieved, there usually follows a slowing and softening of the breath, along with a sense of acceptance, comfort, and relaxation. Laughter and tears are close associates and are often the responses to stress. Contrast the breathing that characterizes laughter or sobbing with the breathing that is typical of stress and it is obvious why the first becomes an antidote to the second. People yawn when tense or fatigued, another example of the body's innate mechanisms for restoring oxygen balance and thus healthy function.

One aspect of good health is the even circulation of energy through the body and the aura. Many difficulties experienced by metaphysical practitioners come about due to neglect of these balances. Many meditators, yoga practitioners, upper-chakra enthusiasts, psychics, intellectuals, and those with sedentary lifestyles forego grounding, lower-chakra activity, and vigorous physical exertion. Symptoms of such neglect include spaciness, lethargy, or nervousness; emotional compaction; disconnection to the body; hypersensitivity; and sometimes depression. Restoring a balance of energy through redirection of the breath and more complete and active use of the body can bring greater vitality to the whole being, upper as well as lower chakras. My body relaxes more fully when the muscles have been used for an activity other than just sitting. My writing flows better after an hour of digging in the garden; perspectives widen and emotional states always improve after a brisk walk.

Without rootedness and balance, the upper chakras and the mind can become overstimulated, subject to delusion and neuroses and lacking integration. Any fixation that ignores the life of the body is ignorant of embodiment's spiritual purpose and potential.

The breath is your most intimate teacher and mirror. If you want an honest reflection of your state of mind, your emotions, your physical condition, or your spiritual reality, look to your breath. Distancing your awareness from breath is distancing yourself from your capacity to be present and clear-intentioned in the now. Working with your breath gives moment-to-moment navigation adjustments that keep you on course, helping you maintain awareness in the most immediate and accessible way possible. The breath is the essence of your interface with life and the thread joining embodied consciousness with the many realms of perception. For the benefits listed below, attention to the breath is the best training a practitioner can receive for honing awareness and establishing a state of health.

- It gives access to the centering required for psychic, healing, or shamanic work.
- It strengthens focus of attention so that extraneous distractions do not interfere with concentration.

- It helps maintain the practitioner's vitality level and minimizes debilitating aftereffects.
- It helps the practitioner deal with traumatic or highly charged situations.
- It deepens and broadens perception.
- It gives a tool for gathering, guiding, focusing, and releasing energy, acting as an energy carrier or energy clearer.
- It gives a pathway for cosmic resource.

As well, when working with another, the practitioner can facilitate the person's active participation by observing and guiding his or her breath.

In the practice of natural spirituality, no tool is more primary than the breath. It is always present and appropriate to use in service to healing. The following suggestions address a few of the breath-related difficulties practitioners may experience.

Trouble deepening the inbreath: This is usually due to constricted exhalation: a full outbreath automatically initiates a deeper inbreath. If there is a habitual tendency for shallow breathing, focus on the exhalation, pushing out the last of the air using the abdominal muscles, diaphragm, and chest. Relax the shoulders. This exaggerated emptying will cause the following inbreath to be deep. With that inbreath, consciously open the chest. (Make sure clothing is not tight at the waist.) After a few cycles of this you won't need to be so willful with the outbreath.

Dizziness following trance: During altered states of consciousness respiration often becomes very light and slow, with long pauses between outbreaths and inbreaths. Transitioning back to ordinary consciousness necessitates taking some moments for bringing respiration/oxygen flow back to a level adequate for the increased demands of body and mind. Blood sugar levels sometimes drop while in altered states, so it is helpful to eat afterward. This also helps dispel dizziness and aids grounding. The most important thing to remember when transitioning out of altered states is to allow time for body/mind reorientation.

Weakness in the voice: Fear, nervousness, lassitude, and lack of full presence all constrict the breath. Practice projecting your voice in private by energetically talking, singing, or chanting. Expand and vitalize the throat, heart, and solar chakras, and relax corresponding areas of the body. Sing loudly with the radio or stereo if your solo voice inhibits you, then turn off the music and see how much more projective your vocalizing is. Practice sustaining a musical note as a way of increasing breath control. Release stress from the jaw, throat, chest, and abdomen using massage, exercise, chakra work, and breath awareness. Consider unresolved communication issues: things said or unsaid, self-doubts, invisibility, fear of causing harm through speech, fear of being harmed for speaking, concern with self-image, using silence as a weapon, using silence as a form of judgment, and so forth.

Inhibition of breath during nightmare or stress: When spiritual practice becomes ingrained it extends into altered states and dreamtime, and is within reach during ordinary situations of stress. Practice that centers on intentional use of the breath and on spiritual application of the voice gives you a transformational tool that is immediately available in constrictive situations. The more familiar you are with that tool, the more easily it can be applied when needed.

Your beliefs are mirrored back to you in times of crisis by your responses to that crisis. When you live inside of a spiritual reality, you reach for what transcends old patterns. Each time you reclaim breath and voice in service to well-being, you strengthen that spiritual reality. Use your breath to calm body and mind. Speak aloud to assert what is true, what is right, what is good.

Establish habits of lucid dreaming that enable you to move and express yourself freely in dreamtime, and to wake when necessary. This involves knowing that you are dreaming when you are in the dream state, and dealing with fear and your responses to fear in both waking and dreaming contexts. Fear, when it is simply held at bay during waking, will find its outlet in dreams. Freedom from fear is achieved through a congruence of spiritual alignment in both waking and dreaming consciousness.

It is interesting that the dream state, conventionally considered a realm of illusion, can be a more accurate mirror of one's fears and beliefs than the conscious waking state. If you feel fear when waking from dreams, attend to your breath immediately, and pray aloud or firmly address any unwelcome energies that have carried over from the dream or altered state.

A ritual form that graphically exemplifies prayerful breath is the Native American pipe ceremony. Within its intricacies of symbolism and gesture rest a fundamental reverence for truth. The core of the ceremony is the breath made visible, the movement of truth using elemental powers and the spiritual focus of prayer.

The pipe is a sort of altar, the prayerful smoke the medicine made upon it. Each part of the pipe embodies an aspect of sacred life. The bowl and stem, when joined, unify dual principles and often honor the particular medicine powers of stones, birds, animals, and trees. Each part of the ceremony describes sacred relationship; smoke is offered to the six Directions and to Spirit. The breath, central to that ceremony, mingles with prayerful intentions put into the pipe, and the breath sends those prayers enlivened into the universe. The life within stone, within herb, within body and mind participates in the truth of Life as breath returns home to itself in the matrix.

three

PRAYER

Prayer has been so long confined to religious definitions that people often think of it as something belonging to dogmas to which they no longer subscribe. Prayer is reconnection. It moves you from a limited, troubled consciousness to a remembrance of what is possible, present, and good.

Prayers of beseechment allow the yearning heart to find a path of realization. Hindrances—obstructive beliefs—are released to make room for well-being to be known. Prayers of gratitude recognize life's gifts. Gratitude is a shifting and redirecting of emotional focus. Like beseechment, it expands receptivity and vitalizes good. All prayers name and empower priorities. A prayerful state of mind is one that knows there is more to reality than the small corner you seem to occupy. It may be difficult to see beyond that corner or to know how to get out of its confines, but prayer can dispell illusions: the doubt, discouragement, forgetfulness, and fear that blinds you to open doors of opportunity and grace. Prayers of invocation are affirmations of the truth of universal interconnection. All beings in the matrix share consciousness, so all are available to your awareness.

Essentially, whether your prayer is beseechment, gratitude, or invocation, it is on some level addressed to Self. It may be Self within the manifested matrix or it may be Self within the unmanifested Mystery, but prayer is not a plea made to some separate power.

Prayer needs to be used with mindfulness of the words being chosen and the feelings that imbue them. Clarity, an attribute of the East, is a key to right use of prayer. Another key is alignment of intention, heart, and mind. Your words and their underlying energies should align to the greatest good for all. Unless your understanding of a situation is all-encompassing—awareness within cosmic consciousness—it is best to generally orient your prayers to the greatest good rather than to specify outcomes. Use prayer as a means of offering your support to a reality of wholeness, love, beauty, and joy.

Prayers of beseechment or of invocation contain the greatest challenge to clarity and wisdom. Prayers of gratitude are the surest means of spiritual alignment. A fourth use of prayer, for banishment or protection, shares the same challenges to clarity that beseechment and invocation present. It may help to look more closely at each of these categories.

Beseechment: These prayers articulate a path of manifestation for desire's intentions. Desire has gotten a bad rap from many systems of organized religion; it is important to realize that desire itself is not an unspiritual thing. Life moves through desire. The more spiritually primal desire is, the less encumbered it is by accumulated energies or shadowy beliefs, the more pure its intentions. Beseechment is the voice of desire, which is why clarity is essential in such prayers. When desire is guided by Spirit's purpose, its articulation gives priority to the manifestation of that purpose. Desire is a primal energy. Given focus of intention and focus of attention, it moves into expression in the universe.

Partnered with desire is receptivity. The active nature of aligned desire needs room to move. This is created by a humbleness in asking. Asking recognizes interdependency. It puts ego in perspective—an important adjustment in the unencumbering of desire. Asking opens the way for reception. Beseechment is often misunderstood by people oriented to concepts of sin, unworthiness, punishment, and separation as pleading to be delivered from judgment. In the old Lakota prayer, "Sacred Mystery, have mercy that the people may live," reconnection is being made. Welcome is being made for an abundance of good. This is not self-flagellation over mortal flaws.

The Lakota are a proud people, yet their prayers of beseechment describe a great depth of receptivity to good through the evocative language of asking.

When you are careful in your word choices and in both your conscious and unconscious intentions, you attend to the implications of what is actually being expressed. You keep in mind that what may seem a positive hope may not be in the larger best interests. It is almost impossible to know what the deepest imperatives of any situation are, so it is wise to avoid presumptions or circumscriptions.

Prayers of beseechment mirror beliefs and feelings and help you see your reality. In the process of spiritual maturing, they help you untangle desire from its shadows and open your life to blessing. Prayers of beseechment choose a path of reunion with well-being.

Invocation: Prayers of invocation usually call upon guides, helpers, totems, ancestors, gods and goddesses, angels, or other presences. Invocation may be for ceremonial occasion or for more informal communion. These prayers assume traffic between the realms: interaction, intercommunication, and the omnipresence of consciousness.

Invocation awakens particular forces that resonate in some essential way with Self. What is called upon emerges in a reality determined and shaped by that resonance. This is the context in which the interaction unfolds, giving encounter its form.

The clarity needed for this kind of prayer is wisdom—knowing what occasions are appropriate situations for such resonances to be called forth. In beseechment you are reminded to be careful of *what* you ask for; in invocation, of *who* you ask for. This responsibility widens if your ceremony includes participants other than yourself. Feckless or rote invocations can call on presences you may not know how to usefully interact with. Calling upon powers, especially collectively charged archetypes, should be done with some awareness of what is being invoked—with some worthwhile and clear intention, and some capacity to relate skillfully with those presences. You probably would not invite a queen or venerated elder or a polar bear to your home without some preparation, sense of purpose, and attentive appropriate response to their presence. Many ceremonialists, however, invoke deities, ancient forces, or totems capriciously or as a matter of form, without sensible purpose, attention, or response. Invocation, like all other aspects of spiritual relationship, is best engaged in with substantial and mutual respect.

Protection: There are several ways to look at invocation and banishment. Often they are seen as prayer directed at outside forces. This view is encouraged by the notion of self as a purely disparate unit. Another view is a psychological perspective of invoked/banished energies as personifications of the individual psyche—mental/emotional amalgamations that are perceived as embodied, separate forms.

A third perspective, neither dualistic nor metaphoric, is a multilayered one. Light is both particle and wave, and all beings, all forces, can also be seen as both unique and inseparable. To invoke Polar Bear is to address something alive and itself, and also to summon a particular resonance within being—to make relationship with the particle and the wave.

In talking about prayer to Self, I am not referring to a separate egoic entity but to the vast power that expresses consciousness through innumerable forms, only some of which are what we think of as material. Through this form of expression you can know yourself as tree, as bird, as waterfall, as mountain, and perhaps as Isis, Kwan Yin, or Pan. Your degree of alignment—the extent of your realized capacity to know this power—determines the depth of those experiences. Resonance broadens the experience; through resonance you can be with tree, or with bird, or waterfall, or mountain, or with Isis, Kwan Yin, or Pan, again to the extent of your realized capacity to participate in larger potentials of consciousness. Being and being with are intrinsic to the true power and use of invocation and banishment.

People who make prayers of protection often perceive themselves (or others) as needing a barrier against threat. This is a purely "particle" view. Great effort can be spent creating and enforcing barriers, and in struggling with reactions to animosity, malice, or aggression. To some degree, shields can be protections from harm, but let us look to the core of these situations, which again are matters of resonance.

When you divide yourself from what threatens you, you are actually locking it in as much as you are locking it out. Just as most energies can only have an effect in accordance with their degree of resonance with some formation inside you, so it is with "bad medicine." Your own shadows are what threaten you; what is unhealed in your own beliefs is what responds in kind to the tuning fork of fear. Malice cannot harm where there is not fear or an answering malice. This is not a battle of light and dark. It is a process of awakening and moving more deeply into understanding. In this process it is wise to look after your safety in the many ways (perhaps including shielding) that are assertive of good. But it is not wise to look outside for what oppresses you, dramatic and engaging as that may be.

Animosity from others can be a teacher calling your attention to patterns within your dance of relationships that do not further peace. What serves is not to blame yourself or play victim, or to fret about perceived injustices, but to seek within your vulnerability for the chord of suffering being struck, and change the negative patterns that perpetuate that pain.

Prayers of protection best come from love, not from fear. These are prayers that resonate with well-being for all. They banish shadows and call upon the strength and courage to be free of oppressive beliefs, whatever their source. Ill wishing has its own natural consequences for the ill wisher. Better to walk with the freedom of love than bind yourself to an ever-escalating game of isolation. Prayer can help you deal with intrusion only when it is used with a straightforward, nonjudgmental, affirming attitude.

Gratitude: Saying thank you is an effective way to change your outlook on and experience of life. Prayers of gratitude are where to go not only when you feel overflowing with grace, but also when you are feeling depressed or deprived.

I used to groan when my mother told me to count my blessings, thinking it a ploy to distract me from rightful grievances. If grievances are what you want to use to base reality upon, then indeed it is a ploy. But if it is more useful to see the water glass as not only half-full (instead of half-empty) but also as an inexplicable grace, then it is simply a shift of perspective. With this shift can be appreciation for the water's presence, happiness in drinking the water, and openness to having the contents of the glass replenished.

Gratitude does not stifle enterprise or sell you short. It expands your awareness of beneficial interaction with the extraordinary gift-edness of each moment. It puts you in touch with your resources on all levels. It lifts your eyes from the gloom and grind of obsession and anxiety about what you crave or think you do not have. Gratitude offers equanimity, if not bliss.

Prayers of gratitude give insight into the world of needs, and into what really nourishes life. Prayers of gratitude are often what are appropriate when you think you need to make prayers of beseech-ment. They return you to center, and from there all else is within reach. A brief, heartfelt thank you each morning for the gift of the new day can change your life.

four

MEDITATION

Someone once told me that meditation is perfect concentration on a perfect thing. While this definition sounds catchy, it catapults meditation to a place of evolvement higher than most people venture toward.

Meditation does indeed involve focus, but for this discussion let us put aside concepts of perfection. If experience of reality is governed by your priority of attention (conscious or unconscious) and your alignment of perspective, then meditation can be a valuable tool because of its influence on attention and perspective. It is part of natural spirituality in its orientation to the primality of breath and its practical integration into daily life.

Look first at priority of attention—this refers to your awareness. At any given moment you are aware of a number of things on a variety of levels. What comprises your perceived reality reflects a prioritizing process: what you notice most is what you choose to notice.

Sitting on a train, there are many things of which to be aware. Your attention could be given to the sound of the wheels or to the passing scenery or to the couple arguing behind you. Or your attention might rest on your thoughts about what to have for lunch, your sadness at leaving your family, your awareness of the vastness of the universe, or any number of other possibilities. Each of these thoughts carries its attendant array of choices for response. This is where alignment of perspective—point of view—comes in.

If it is the arguing couple that catches your attention, for example, your response—which is shaped by your perspective, generally a habitual one—might be to recall your own conflicts. Or the arguing might make you realize how glad you are to have a harmonious partnership with someone. It might stimulate irritation if you are trying to rest, or embarrassment at having people exhibit such intense behavior in public. As well, it might awaken your compassion for the struggles of human relationship.

The person sitting next to you may have her attention on the click of the train's wheels, with a perspective that it is a comforting, pleasing rhythm. So, as you perhaps suffer in the reality of conflict and tension, the person beside you relaxes in her reality of enjoyment.

How does meditation influence these aspects of experience? First, meditation settles the mind on the breath. This puts you in the now of your consciousness, bringing cessation to forward and backward projections, skittering thoughts, and unconscious reactivity. From this centering you can choose a priority of attention; the centering itself aligns perspective with the simplicity and power of the breath. Thus aware and aligned, you are afforded a greater clarity of perception and are more in touch with your choices (and their implications) in the matter of response. Thus aware and aligned, you can move with more freedom and precision and with a more useful basis of intention.

Meditation establishes habits of calm and strengthens attention span and depth of concentration. It helps you disengage from patterns that lock your perspective into negative alignments. It also teaches you about transitoriness.

Thoughts come and go. Emotions arise and recede. Energy is always on the move. Reality's relative continuum is constantly changing. When attention is focused in the now and reaction is stilled, the mind can observe the arrival and passing of thoughts, feelings, impulses, and sensations. It realizes that all these are transitory. This realization can release you from bondage to (though not necessarily from caring about) what is not enduring.

To see an idea or an emotion or a condition as inherently subject to change is to know that its main perpetuation is your insistence on prolonging it. You can cling to things or you can disentangle yourself (or refrain from entangling) or you can move transformatively. Knowing the truth of change, you can choose a path of positive participation. There is no need to be fettered by mental conditioning. Just because you believed certain things or responded in certain ways in the past does not necessitate your continuing to do so. Now is now—the opportunity for change is always present. A tool that helps you know and remember this is a resource worth cultivating.

Visualization involving active or passive imagery is also a resource of the East. Though in itself a major topic, the aspect of visualization explored here is its implementation within meditation.

In *The Spirit of Place* I wrote at greater length about visualization. An important point made in that book and reiterated here is this: There is a difference between visualization and shamanic states of consciousness/trance. Most journeying that lay people engage in is actually more within the strata of visualization than of shamanic trance. I write this not to belittle but to further understanding of this work, and thus to encourage its most effective application.

The imagery of visualization is a projection of the mind. The more relaxed the state of consciousness, the more freely the imagery flows, perhaps tapping deep wells of the subconscious. This kind of visualization often begins with a set context or intention but no pre-arranged story line. A more directive form of visualization is that of guided imagery, which selects from a narrower stream in order to produce more specific effects. Most exact of all is the visualization used in meditation.

A person practiced in meditation allows thoughts, feelings, and sensations to rise and subside, to go through their cycles without engaging with them. Focus is either on, within, or beneath the breath or its places of passage, or it is on some other particularity such as a mantra, koan, or chakra. The microcosm being a gate to the macrocosm, complete concentration on a particular something can open paradoxically into an experience of allness, or of void, or of other transcendent states. This may be true of concentration on anything if focus is strong enough; however, the focus points traditionally used in meditation are keys to certain kinds of transcendence, and so have specific purposeful effects on movement of consciousness (and also on the body and aura).

Meditation is full of paradox: letting go in order to focus; focusing in order to let go. Meditation is at once full of cunning maneuvers to circumvent or exhaust the mind's habits, and of simplicities that confound the mind's cognizant modes. It is something a child can do, yet lifetimes can be spent exploring its potentials.

Active visualization is sometimes used in meditation. Trance, meditation, dreaming, and visualization are all different activities, though aspects of some may be used within others, such as visualization within meditation. Active visualization chooses an image or series of images as a blueprint for the expression of consciousness. In traditional meditation, this blueprint is often of the chakra system, pranic channels, or a deity form, the imagery based on teachings that describe them. Utilizing breath control, and grounded in the power of knowledge and belief within meditative focus, the practitioner aligns her reality with the visualized model and thus vitalizes it. In this state transformative work can be done, and realization of the potentials of consciousness expanded or reinforced.

Affirmative imagery in itself is therapeutic and can help change beliefs and life experiences. The visualization used by meditators goes beyond that and takes committed practice and skill, but both are part of a continuum of application.

Some friends and I had firsthand experience with active visualization within meditation as used by a traditional Buddhist. A Tibetan Rinpoche traveling in North America agreed to see a friend of mine with cancer, in hopes that the Rinpoche might help in my friend's healing. The Rinpoche spoke to us through another monk who acted as interpreter. During his examination of our friend, the Rinpoche shifted from a healing intention to preparation for death; though nothing was said to indicate this, the change in his agenda was apparent.

The Rinpoche requested that we participate in what he was doing by meditatively visualizing a particular deity he described. He said he (the Rinpoche) would become that deity. Using his well-worn prayer beads, the Rinpoche spoke to our friend in the wheelchair as the other monk and we four North Americans earnestly visualized the deity. I soon became aware of the deity's attributes emanating from the Rinpoche; this appeared to be direct transformation rather than invocation. When he was finished, the Rinpoche tossed grains of rice on our friend and on us. He spoke for some time through the interpreter, and gave our friend some medicines and sanctified objects to ease his suffering. It was a simple and extraordinary experience, one I reflect on often.

What is the difference—or is there a difference—between using visualization for transformation in this meditative way, and the shift into totemic forms that can occur in shamanic traditions? In terms of the medicine wheel, the meditative mode is of the East direction and trance is of the West. It seems to me that the Eastern meditative path uses the mind to guide transformation, and the Western trance path uses transformation to guide the mind.

In meditation, transcendence comes about through discipline of attention and perspective; in trance it comes through surrender to the experience of no boundaries. Both recognize limitlessness. The Rinpoche focuses and visualizes, using mind transcendently. The shaman drums, dances, or partakes of consciousness-altering plants in order to disintegrate the ordinary. In the East, medicine wheel emphasis is on mind/enlightenment; in the West it is on feeling/intuition. But both the skilled meditator and the competent shaman can work transformation through the actualized powers they visualize or invoke, because they are operating in realms where energy goes beyond imagery. In these states, their paradigms of reality are greatly expanded, not sabotaged by ego concepts or beliefs in separation.

The Rinpoche was quite matter-of-fact about becoming a deity; likewise, a traditional shaman may find it expedient to perhaps become a bear. Neither works within wishfulness or fantasy. They enact transformation. Imagery may be part of this process, but it is used within an altered perception that links imagery with a larger matrix of reality.

five

BELIEF

In natural spirituality your orientation is to what is primary, as close to center as possible. With this orientation you do not get distracted by the packaging around basic energies. Natural spirituality is concerned with core truths and foundations of power and understanding.

The chapter on meditation looked at priority of attention and alignment of perspective. Perspective is built upon beliefs, which are usually formed early in life. If these beliefs are not tightly held, they may be influenced by differing notions or by personal realizations, both of which can change perspective. My imagery of a belief is of a chemical compound: elements of knowledge or perception bound together by emotional charges to create mental formations.

These formations become your references for perspective, for personal reality. Transformational spiritual practices are those that change belief. Whatever the practice—and all religions have these somewhere in their history—the process that takes place is the undoing of belief compounds. This process is sometimes initiated spontaneously during traumatic situations (and its aftereffects unpredictable) or it may be part of intentional healing or ceremonial activities. The energies released in this undoing may, in the course of habit, reform into the same compound, or they may be rearranged into different beliefs, or they may be dispersed to be used otherwise. All profound changes in one's conditional reality include belief transformations.

Beliefs can be complex compounds. If you can identify useful core aspects of a belief, you can free those from what burdens them. For example, your belief that parenting is a worthwhile commitment may become loaded with guilt about neglecting your spouse, or with religious compulsion about being fruitful and multiplying, or with resentment held over from your own unhappy childhood. If a belief has a useful core, it can be freed by dissolving the structures surrounding it. If the basic belief is not useful, the entire compound can be transformed.

In working with your beliefs it is necessary to identify or create core tenets to give guidance to your perspective and a nucleus for energy freed through transformative process to gather around. These core beliefs can be strengthened each time you dismantle unproductive formations by directing the released energy into the useful beliefs. Realigning energy is what change on all levels is about. Realigning energy at the level of belief is more than a temporary fix, and reaches into all aspects of experience.

How can this process be enacted in daily life through the simple practices of natural spirituality? One way of addressing this is to use the resources of the medicine wheel. Each of the Directions offers specific approaches.

In the East is awareness of belief. Intellectual contemplation and understanding are the East's ways of interfacing with belief. The resultant action in terms of transformation is the formulation and vitalization of new intentions. The tools for this are breath, prayer, meditation, affirmation, visualization, and smudging. Awareness is used to reroute energy to the formulated positive intentions, positive perspectives, and positive feelings.

In the South, belief is mirrored in relationship. As opposed to the East's contemplative mode, in the South interaction is the arena for understanding and change. The chosen movement would be making alliances that support transformation. The South's tools are the resources of relationship and totemic alignment, as well as the use of fire or light. Here you actively work to create healthy relationships by changing your behavior within interactions.

In the West, belief is experienced through its emotional charge. The interface with the energies of the West is through introspection, and the resultant transformative action would be to deal with fear. In doing so you are then able to let go of the charges that hold negative compounds together, and the freed mental formations can be rearranged or released. The tools for this are altered states of consciousness, ceremony, emotional exhaustion, emotional shifts, and the use of water. You positively apply the fluidity of emotional states to dissolve fixity and to nourish love, compassion, and transcendent acceptance.

In the North, belief manifests through physical circumstance. It is tracked through its symptoms: health conditions, living conditions, financial states, and other material indicators. The positive transformative action is to address habits and contexts. The tools are healing modalities, right livelihood, service, physical practices such as yoga and t'ai chi, bodywork, wisdom about food, elements of lifestyle, appropriate location, and work with stones and crystals as patterning matrices. Here you can actualize change through balance and health.

The East's transformative expression is active, clear intelligence; the South's is joyful interaction and good relationship; the West's is a fearless heart and freedom to grow; and the North's is embodied well-being.

Daily attention to the resources of each Direction offers opportunity for beliefs to be identified, understood, and transformed. Beliefs about self are usually the stickiest of all, and will be discussed in greater depth in the chapter on Self (part two).

Primal forces such as desire are often adversely obscured or distorted by troubled beliefs. In the process of sorting and clearing—of looking more closely at your mental formations—you may be able to liberate powerful primal energies and apply them more naturally. Suppose your relationship to the force of gravity (which is a form of desire) became encumbered by links to evil, sin, violence, or dark compulsions. How would this change your relationship to the force of gravity? Consider how other forces of desire—physical, mental, emotional, and spiritual—could be well used if cleared of aberrance.

Distilling belief does not imply embracing dogmatism. I am not suggesting that you surround yourself with a bulwark of simplistic positivity. The points I am making here are several:

- That beliefs determine one's personal paradigm.
- That transformation occurs only when beliefs change or are aligned with positive, productive intentions.
- That it is more useful to work with core beliefs than with their accumulated complexities.
- That in order for a belief to change it must be recognized as a belief and not an ultimate truth.

Sometimes you find core beliefs at odds with each other. To have clarity of perspective or a particular unfoldment of reality, such conflict must be resolved. This is achieved by dissolving whatever beliefs are counter to your chosen alignment. (Conceivably there are times when it is fine to leave contradictory beliefs in place, as long as you realize the effect this will have on your experience.)

Beware the needy habit of turning opinions, observations, or impressions into beliefs. It is much easier to move flexibly within the realm of opinions, observations, and impressions than within the more entrenched, emotionally invested world of beliefs. You do not need a lot of beliefs—just a few good ones, and those regularly reconsidered.

Fixed beliefs go along with the need to be right; willingness to change reduces suffering and allows growth. This is not to say that core beliefs are not to be taken seriously, or that you should blithely uproot truths that support well-being. The ground you stand on can be honored—just be aware of what it consists of, and why/how you defend it.

Consciously living your beliefs lets you see their elements. It is the best way to know their worth and to express integrity. If you are honest and attentive, it is also the obvious way to recognize your own contradictions. Sometimes you may think you are aligned with one belief only to find yourself following the dictates of another. Perhaps you are unwilling or unable to see that it is a conflicting belief, and not outside circumstances, that is undermining your desired path. That conflicting belief can be a subtle dictator: something from younger years, or something disguised as being compatible with the desired alignment when it actually is not, or something you do not want to admit believing even to yourself.

Once identified, the energetic charge of this belief will likely intensify if you try to transform it. This is true with anything touched by fear—and there is always some form of fear in an unhealthy charge. You may experience feelings of constriction when you begin transforming this belief's source of continuance, which is fear. As you persist in this process, disempowering the unwanted belief and empowering your core truths, the agitation will diminish.

As with physical healing, there is often a crisis period as the energies of conflicting beliefs are released and realigned, and it helps to keep this in mind as the shift occurs. The feelings of constriction can narrow your outlook and challenge your courage and commitment. During any work with transformation of belief, remember to be compassionate with this struggle, but also determined. Each step unlocks perception and serves well-being.

six

PERCEPTION

A matrix is something out of which something else is created or emerges. I think of the cosmos as a matrix emerging from Mystery, a matrix that has both manifested and unmanifested aspects. The manifested matrix includes the universe of forms—some easier to perceive than others—to which our world's web of life belongs. Because of the weblike interrelationship of life, perception can move through all its strands—a process that expands Self awareness. (Self/no self is a debate of religious semantics. For the purposes of this book, self is a "particle," egoic truth, and Self is a "wave" truth; see the chapter on Prayer. Absolute Truth is not the provenance of this book.)

Consciousness-altering drugs or psychotropic plants often lead people into transcendent expansions of Self-awareness, wherein they feel themselves within every blade of grass, in every grain of stardust; they feel themselves as an awakened part of all. Loosed from egoic (particle) consciousness, perception can go anywhere in the web, and perhaps beyond.

One of the most important aspects of transcendent consciousness is the absence of fear. Fear, in one shape or another, shadows much of conventional consciousness. It lurks, it seizes, it threatens peace at every turn. The particle self is a vulnerable and lonely being; all particle selves, of whatever species or kind, sometimes suffer fear. It is in the response to fear that you can establish transcendence. The particle choosing love reenters perception of the wave. Separation, isolation, fearfulness, anxiety dissolve in the presence of connectedness. Love is always accessible in transcendent consciousness.

Perception can occur, then, as wave awareness. It can also take place in aligned particle consciousness. This harks back to the chapter on prayer, and the experiences of being and being with. Within alignment you can approach uniqueness with uniqueness, and commune on that level with other forms in the web. This is sometimes part of shamanic practice.

Perception differs from projection. A friend told me he knows that he is perceiving by the surprise of what emerges from the encounter, and that he is projecting by the way insights reiterate what he already supposed. This illustrates one mechanism of projection—that it prevents an expansion of perspective. The projections are beliefs, assumptions, and oftentimes emotions that you are either trying to disassociate from or include others within. Aligned perception opens and extends. Projection obscures; it is a mirror of belief.

Projection can be a useful mirror if you are not confused about what is occurring. Projection can help you see more distinctly beliefs and feelings that elude the contemplative eye. Used this way, projection becomes a kind of perception; but it is a perception of personal patterns, not perception of the larger matrix.

Sometimes projection totally preempts perception, and sometimes it simply accompanies it. The latter happens when perception—usually of the particle-to-particle variety—is followed by an infusion of projected emotion. For example, your communion with an elderly, weathered tree might bring up feelings about aging and dying. Your perception of the tree then becomes overlaid with the projected feelings that you may or may not attribute to the tree rather than to yourself. Honoring and participating in connectedness while accepting each being's integrity of perspective is intrinsic to right relationship. Perception is servant of both connection and uniqueness.

What perceives? The senses, physical and subtle, are part of perception. The body perceives. The mind perceives. I think the heart perceives as well, because love is the medium of the matrix, and the heart knows love's language best of all. In working with the manifested matrix it is helpful to use all these ways of perceiving.

Pick up a stone (with its permission) and examine it. Become quiet and attentive. Rest your eyes on its color and design; follow its topography with your fingers; feel its texture, temperature, weight, and density. Smell its mineral-ness. Taste it, perhaps, or taste its fragrance. Listen to its story. Feel the resonances—let perception flow through the strands of connectedness. Open your heart to the heart of the stone—to the deepness, to its song. All things have heart; through this, love stirs, awakening desire to Be.

The way of perception asks for stillness. If I invited you to tell me about yourself and then half-ignored you, I would not learn much. Being quiet, being still, and being open help you not only to be attentive, but also to attend with respect and with heart.

Perception in the manifested martrix can occur without the presence of the physical form of that which you want to contact. The form, or even part of the form, (such as a bird's feather or a mountain's rock), are aspects of the spectrum of manifestation, but their absence does not preclude connection. Focus on the resonance of that bird or mountain will guide perception. Imagery or invocation may be useful, if you are moving within an awareness of the matrix and your perception is attuned.

Sometimes you open to the matrix in prayer or with intention to address some need, not knowing what form will resonate with that prayer/intention. For this to be successful, perception must be a widely receptive yet centered awareness.

One of the most frequent requests made of me is to "look into" situations. I may be looking into an illness, a chakra, a dream, an incident, a behavior pattern, an object, a space, or any number of things. The feedback I give may include insights based on knowledge, observation, intuition, or comparison to similar situations. I try to identify these sources both to myself and to the asker.

The level of looking-into that is most particularly valued is that of perception within the subtle realms. In accessing these I ask for whatever is right to know to be made known to me. Sometimes what follows is inexplicable to me but makes perfect sense to the asker.

I do not remember when or how this capacity to access such knowing developed, but it gradually became something used with greater attention, and for others. I cannot teach anyone how to do it—like breathing, it is a natural function that can be applied to various needs—but it may be useful to describe some of its characteristics.

Looking-into operates in the cosmic here and now, because it can be done at distances and touches on past, present, and future. With experience I have learned to sense what dimension of reality is being presented. It requires letting go of preconceptions, vested interests, and performance pressure. I do not find this difficult, though it is not because I am an "evolved" person; there are occasions of other sorts on which I impose preconceptions, vested interests, and my need to please.

Letting go consists of closing my eyes, relaxing, silently stating a request to know what is right to be known, opening to the manifested and unmanifested matrices, and being attentive. I feel my consciousness shift—sometimes it jolts, oftentimes it is a feeling of suddenly but gently breaking through a skin of ice and sinking into deep, vast waters. At that point the usual mental/emotional business simply seems to stop at some threshold as perception is released into the subtle realms. This process of release is facilitated by knowing it is Spirit, not Loren, who guides medicine work. The process is so familiar that it often operates spontaneously; usually a momentary disorientation accompanies the shift of consciousness. This happens when the process has been more deliberately entered into as well.

If trance, in the West of the medicine wheel, is defined as a state of transcendent receptivity, and meditation, in the East of the medicine wheel, is regarded as state of transcendent focus, the process of looking-into seems to integrate elements of both. Like many, this process is most challenging to apply to yourself or to those with whom you are closest. The difficulty lies in the feelings that influence openness and clarity. If you have anxieties about what might be received, you may end up with barriers preventing your perception from moving freely, or preconceptions may obscure your knowing.

A last perceptive mode to be touched on in this chapter is that of using the manifested matrix to access the unmanifested. This is like using the peripheral stations on the medicine wheel to reach its center. Since consciousness is pervasive, its source can be found through any of its manifestations. If you return to that stone you were examining earlier in the chapter, you can see this process taking place. You have entered the stone through the gate of its manifested form to its essence—from expressive being to essential being that is still particular, still unique—the Mystery's thought that is that stone.

From there you can move deeper yet, tracing that thought to the Mind of Mystery, the unmanifested matrix from which all arises and returns, the formless consciousness that dreams us. Experience of the unmanifested matrix may not come easily or often—it cannot be forced. It may happen in a moment of egoless communion; it may open within meditation; it may catch you completely by surprise. There are infinite doorways into infinity.

seven

WHEEL WORKINGS

The following are six wheel workings that demonstrate a variety of ways to move on the medicine wheel, and that emphasize different aspects of the wheel and of the sorts of work compatible with this mandala. These workings are most effectively done with an actual medicine wheel large enough to walk through and around, to encourage a physical sense of movement and change. In this final chapter of part one, these workings bring attention back to where we began, with a map to help us journey.

To begin, set up a wheel in a sacred manner and invoke the Six Powers; the spirits of place; the ancestors, guides, and helpers; and the blessing of the Mystery. Smudge yourself and the wheel before each working.

Chakra Working

This is a counterclockwise movement on the wheel for deepening understanding of the directional elements and for clearing and strengthening the chakras.

Begin in the North. Ground yourself and orient Northward. Focus on your first chakra. Sustaining focus, link the chakra with the North Direction, using your breath to draw in elemental energy from the North (mineral energy) and to release anything needing to be cleared from the first chakra.

When this is completed to the degree that feels right for now, let your focus come to rest for a few moments. Send a prayer of gratitude to the North, then move along the circle of the wheel to the West.

Again orient yourself facing outward. Focus on the second chakra and link it with water, the elemental energy of the West. Nourish and clear this chakra. Rest a moment in gratitude, and move to the South.

In the South, repeat this process focusing on the third chakra and the fire element. Turn then to the East, repeating this process with the fourth chakra and the air element.

Move to the North, completing your circuit, and from there go to the center of the wheel. Orient to the Earth below you, and work with the fifth chakra, then align the sixth chakra with the Sky. Last, focus on the seventh chakra and the wheel's center. When this is finished, open your focus to include the whole chakra system and circulate energy throughout it. Make your final prayer of gratitude to the Mystery, ending this working.

Totem Working

This working is for nourishing your relationships with your totems and understanding more about their associations with particular Directions.

Lie down in your wheel with your feet toward the center and your head toward the East. Close your eyes and relax. Shift into an altered state of consciousness, using whatever helps you to achieve this. Call on your totem from the East. If you do not have one, call on an ally or on a sacred being you associate with the East. Hold a contact object, if this helps you. Convey your intention to understand this being's correlation with its directional home.

Receive whatever insights the totem offers. Ask if there is anything needing to be known by you at this time. Nurture your relationship through this encounter. Express gratitude and appreciation.

Move to the South, with your head toward the Direction and feet toward the center, and repeat this same process orienting to this new

Direction. Do the same in the West and in the North. Each time feel the connection between the manifested matrix in the Direction and the unmanifested matrix in the center, as well as your connection with the totems. Finish the working by returning to the East.

Self-Perspective Working

This is a movement for bringing insight into your beliefs about yourself, and for using directional focuses to work with those beliefs.

Begin with a paper and pen. Sit in the East and list ten words to describe yourself. When the list is complete, organize the words into directional categories: North—words that indicate your physical appearance or roles you enact, such as parent, truck driver, and so on; East—qualities of conscious mind, or ones that emphasize conscious use of the mind; South—personality traits, idiosyncrasies, qualities of ego; and West—any words that indicate aspects of the unconscious, the heart, or emotions.

Examine this arrangement. Is there a predominant Direction? Any empty categories? What is the pattern? What words are positive to you? Which ones are negative? Where do these perspectives of yourself come from? Is this list different than it would have been a year ago? If so, what caused the changes?

Put the list down and orient yourself outward to the East. Call to mind the self-descriptive words you put in the East category. Take these words one at a time and, using the resources of the East, either clear the words of any influences they have on your truth or self, or strengthen your relationship with the qualities they represent. Another possibility is to move these qualities to a different octave of expression, for example, to shift from "smart" to "intelligent," strengthening your relationship to the latter.

When finished, move to the South and repeat the same process, using the words from your list that correspond to the South. Move next to the West, and then the North. Complete the circle by returning to the East. This time face inward to the center. Make a prayer of thanks to the Directions, and state an intention to forthwith address self-perspective more flexibly and in alignment with the unfoldment that best expresses spiritual growth.

Cross-Quarter Working

Instead of the directional stations, here you commune with the cross-quarters or winds. This working is best done with accompanying drum and rattle sounds. Give yourself plenty of time in each cross-quarter, working within an altered state if possible. The cross-quarter wheel is often used as a healing wheel or to bring change or movement—to clear your path.

Begin in the Southeast, facing outward. Greet that Direction and orient yourself to it. Begin to drum strongly and with a vigorous pace. With eyes opened or closed, see a blue wind coming from the Southeast. It is a steady, warm, bracing wind. It exudes confidence and passion. Feel it. Feel it on your face, moving through you, helping you in whatever way is needed. Feel it circling you, circling and removing obstruction from around you. (Let the drumming intensify.) The wind circles four times then moves away, returning to the Southeast. Watch it go. Let the drumming fade in volume but retain its pace. When the wind has disappeared in the distance, stop the drumming. Offer gratitude.

Move to the Southwest, facing outward. Greet the Direction and orient to it. Begin to drum with a variable volume and pace. See a black wind coming toward you. It is a hot, gusting, unpredictable wind, primal and impersonal. Feel it on your face, moving through you, helping you in whatever way is needed. It circles you four times, removing obstructions, and slowly withdraws into the distance. Again, adjust the drumming to the wind's retreat. Offer thanks, and move on.

In the Northwest repeat the procedure, but use a rattle. This is a yellow wind, a gentle, cool breeze that foretells rain. It is refreshing and nourishing.

In the Northeast is the white wind. Use a soft heartbeat drumming for this. It is a cold, swirling, spiraling wind. It carries mystery and acceptance.

At the end of this working give yourself some time to integrate the movements, and to reorient to ordinary consciousness. Cross-quarter work is meant to be unsettling.

Roadwork

Most of these movements have involved the wheel's perimeter. The roads are often neglected in people's relationship with the wheel. This working is one of many ways of moving on the roads. It correlates with the description of transformation in the chapter on belief. The physical movement on the wheel is a surprisingly powerful aspect of the work.

Begin in the East, facing West. Orient to where you are. Meditate until a negative belief arises and is recognized as one you want to transform at this time.

Move across the wheel to the West, and face East. Shift into an altered consciousness. (Use drumming here, if it is helpful.) Allow the structure of the belief to dissolve. When its energy is released from structure, move to the wheel's center and face South. Align the freed energy with a core belief you want to reinforce. Center it in yourself.

Move to the South and face North. Connect with the allies in the matrix who support that core belief. (Drum here also, if helpful.) Ask those allies to aid you.

Move to the North and face South. Connect with your body, and with how that core belief can be expressed through daily living. Abide with this for a while, strengthening commitment.

Move to the center. Integrate being and doing. Feel the interplay of the roads and Directions. Center yourself. Offer gratitude.

Move to the East, facing Center. Look at the original, negative belief. Has it changed?

Wheel of Intention's Fulfillment

This last working is a classic perimeter movement conducted as a pipe ceremony. In it you use a prayer pipe, or tobacco or herbs rolled into papers. It loosely corresponds to the description in the first chapter on the medicine wheel.

You begin in the East, with intention. Spend some time formulating this intention. Make sure it can be clearly expressed and that it is worthy of fulfillment.

Take your tobacco (or other herb) in hand. Speak your intention, charging the tobacco with it. Put some of the tobacco aside, and with the rest load the pipe or roll your prayer smoke, continuing to pray aloud.

Carry your pipe/prayer smoke to the South and set it along the South–North road with the bowl touching the South stone. Take the remaining tobacco or herbs and, in your smudge bowl or other suitable container (or in a fire or stove placed in the South), burn this tobacco with prayers to your allies for help in fulfilling your intention. Align the intention to right relationship in the web of life.

Carry the pipe/prayer smoke to the West and set it along the East–West road, bowl touching the West stone. You may want drumming at this point. Have a vessel of consecrated water waiting here. In the West, confront your fears and negative beliefs concerning your intention. Use the water to help clear and move you in this process.

Proceed to the North, setting the pipe/prayer smoke along the South–North road, bowl touching the North stone. Have a receptive stone or crystal here. Ask it to help you align your energies with the manifestation of your intention. Work with the stone or crystal as needed.

Return to the East. In a sacred manner smoke the pipe or prayer herbs, honoring all Directions, all sacred beings, and the Mystery. Pray that your intention be purified and brought into right relationship with the well-being of all, and expressed in the universe in alignment with that well-being. Send your smoke, then take the ashes from it and from your smudge bowl, and any water remaining from your West work, and give them to the elements. As you do so, release your attachment to outcomes. Clear the stone or crystal you used in the North, and put it away, with gratitude. So ends this working.

Life song
of the desert—
carried on
buzzard wing
circling,
on small path
of lizard
patterned,
the cactus people
listen
mountain to mountain
winds travel.
Desert song
prowls the oasis
hums like
thin gold
through
abandoned mines,
rolls like
tumbleweed
to the sea.

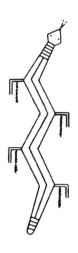

PART TWO

South
Fire

one

SELF

South is where relationship dances and manifested consciousness explores its uniqueness, its particularity. South is the realm of encounter and interaction. Here particle self experiences difference, and that experience informs and is informed by belief.

Particle self often forgets wave Self, and in doing so falls into egotism and suffers from illusion of separation. The shadow side of perceiving difference is a divisive sense of otherness that projects fear. This fear goes by many names: racism, sexism, species arrogance, bigotry, selfishness, hatred, miserliness, jealousy, control, alienation, ridicule, revenge, scapegoating, demonization, and so on.

When differences are not divorced from connectedness, they are instead seen as diversity—aspects of each person's uniqueness that enrich wholeness and begin to describe manifest potential.

Ego has a useful function. Because it is concerned with individual manifestation, when ego is healthy it helps look after the well-being of the body and individual circumstances. It participates in the individual's integrity and is wary of intrusion, abuse, and aggression. Ego keeps its eye on the survival and prospering of the particle self. It expresses idiosyncrasies and experiences singularity.

This experience would not be possible, however, without the context of life's web. Singularity is relative to multiplicity. Without a group, individuality is meaningless. Ego's experience comes through relationship.

This can open the way for egotism: the comparing and competing that breeds discontent, dominance, victimization, oppressive hierarchy, and self-doubt. Beliefs collect around these themes and form tendencies that shape not only individual perspective but societal norms as well. Spiritual reality becomes obscured by assumptions of separation that turn people against each other, and thus against themselves (and Selves). Violence is always suicide. Another aspect of egotism that prevails in modern society is the separation people feel between personal needs and the needs of others, and the sense of having to choose to fulfill either one or the other.

Self-esteem is a focus of modern psychotherapy. It is an ego issue, so is subject to the tendency of ego to be heavily influenced by comparisons. Interactions that yield positive comparison contribute to self-esteem, and interactions that are bummers usually produce low self-esteem because of the beliefs about self they engender and reflect. This narrows into a perpetual cycle of interactions reinforcing those beliefs that in turn create the pattern of experience.

Many people strive for high self-esteem. While this may be valuable to the ego (if it is truly achieved and not just a veneer), it is still a perception of limited self, not of Self. Because ego is so involved with the particle perspective of comparison, measure, and competitive well-being, it is always vulnerable to encounters that assail self-esteem. People with great assurance have less difficulty maintaining high self-regard, but most people in today's world have undergone wounding of the ego. The wounded ego can feel big self-esteem or great self-loathing (or will fluctuate between the two). The absorption in ego lures consciousness away from remembrance of a larger reality of Self, and is unhealthy.

Rather than wrestle, perhaps interminably, with issues of esteem, it may be more useful to heal the wounded ego through transcendent awareness. Respect for Self, embodied in right relationship, will naturally include respect for self once it is realized that self is part of love's matrix. To paraphrase Cherokee teacher Dyhani Ywahoo, "Have some confidence, proceed with some certainty; you have been given a body, given breath, stop questioning your worthiness." Life is sacred. You are alive; you are a sacred being. Connect with that sacredness. Look for it in every beating heart, in every form life touches. Let your particle self shine in the light-wave that is the illumined cosmos. Be alive in the sacred, and let the sacred live through you. Awareness of Self is awareness of love. In rejoining self to Self, ego returns to healthy function. You realize that there is a difference between feeling one with everything and negating self through trying to satisfy other people's expectations.

Injurious habits of self-belief plague most practitioners. They are nothing to be ashamed of (another injurious habit). It may help to more appropriately employ discernment. Discernment is a function of intelligence; too often it is shuttled into judgment. Discernment itself is usually sufficient for the task of sorting through what you are presented with. Judgment can load discernment with emotional values that invoke guilt or blame. It makes heavy drama out of a simple perceptive process. It can impede transformative clarity and movement.

When I am in the garden picking tomatoes for canning, I sort the suitable fruits from the unsuitable ones. When I come across one with a decayed spot or other blight on it I toss it (with gratitude for its efforts and gifts) into the compost pile. I do not sneer at it or vilify it or disparage its essential tomato character. This is a process of discernment—it is compassionate and clear-sighted.

Discernment applies to how you look at self as well. When something is noticed that is not suitable to right relationship or joyful being or intelligent action, you can simply recognize its unsuitability and transform (compost) it, instead of making a judgmental production out of the situation. Judgment binds your energies instead of freeing them. Sometimes you may catch yourself in the midst of judging yourself, and then get in even deeper by judging yourself for judging yourself. Humor helps—just stop, and have a laugh at habit's contortions. Sweep it away and start over. Breathe. Now is now. Judgment means that when you catch yourself doing or thinking something from outmoded patterns, you punish yourself emotionally. Discernment means that when you catch yourself you say "Aha," and make a change.

This relates to interactions with others also. Focusing on discernment instead of judgment gives space for you and others to become free from negative patterns. Discernment includes acceptance, and so bypasses judgment's constrictions—the deadening of possibility at a barrier of belief. With acceptance, movement can continue on its path of transformation.

What most people are conditioned to define as change in themselves is really just a rearrangement of the same furniture in ego's house. There are certainly teachings offered within this activity, but this may become frustrating if your intention is a larger shift in experience. The arena of ego is where you are occupied with self-esteem, sensitive to praise or criticism, influenced by childhood patterns, find personal needs at odds with the needs of others, define yourself as an individual and through individuality, and concern yourself with issues of control and boundaries.

The resources of the South (and the South–North road) offer not only assistance in the arena of ego, but in enabling self to integrate with Self. This gives reference, through relationship, to a reality that transcends or resolves the dualistic frustrations of ego orientation. Relationship is where this me/you dance is enacted most graphically, giving mirror to ego and context to the experience of self and Self.

One day driving in my truck to town I was pondering what to do about a situation, looking at various options. Some options I dismissed because of challenges they presented to "the way I am." "I couldn't do that," I mentally responded to one of those stressful possibilities. "I'm too shy." Suddenly I realized that shyness is not the issue. It is not a matter of shifting to the opposite of shyness, or of trying to become some other sort of individual, or of conquering shyness. All those are just rearrangements and strategies within ego. It is a matter of transcendent awareness of Self. In that sudden remembrance of the obvious—that what you experience of self is dependent in each moment on how you are thinking of self—I had a transcendent expansion that freed me entirely from patterns of self-identity. I experienced a marvelous feeling of lightness and joy.

Knowing that the issue is not shyness versus boldness, for example, allows you to go beyond endless grappling in the ego arena and heal yourself through the knowing of Self. This does not make you ego-less; it simply puts things into a perspective of larger options. With this perspective you base your choices on your alignment to right action, not on the self-limiting beliefs clustered around ego.

When that state of transcendent awareness I experienced in my truck shifted to again include ego consciousness, I felt a change, a loosening of constrictive belief structures. Each loosening of this sort is part of transformation. The experience of freedom encourages change. It reminds me of the feeling in early pregnancy when nothing much shows on the outside, but inside you knowingly carry a seed that grows and manifests and will change your life forever.

Transcendent awareness gives you truths that can be integrated and expressed in daily life. Wave and particle consciousness have the same source. Clearing beliefs that relegate you to an egoic self-knowing gives you passage into extended consciousness.

As a spiritual practitioner it is vital to do your South work, to look directly at ego and self-belief. Egotism looms large in the world of practitioners who have not faced those beliefs that manifest through relationship with others and relationship with power. Some practitioners bluster along using egotism as an aspect of leadership; some try to disguise egotism as spiritual authority; some make it a device of humbleness or justify it as a survival tool. With ego considered so taboo, it is difficult for practitioners to address its presence, much less its undue influence. It is necessary to retrieve the original functions and respectful understandings of such things as ego, desire, and the physical body. It will be easier to deal with aberrance around these once their essential purposes are embraced.

When a practitioner has experiences of transcendent awareness before this work with ego has been attended to, there can be confusion resulting in the attachment of divinity to the egoic self. This is a confusion of self with Self (or with Mystery), and manifests as a practitioner who feels personal ownership of power or of spiritual gifts. This sense of personal grandeur and control can be a perilous egotism producing flawed or harmful expressions of spiritual gifts.

Another possibility is that transcendent awareness will result in a practitioner walling-off ego, dividing self from Self because of a sense of irreconcilability. This ends up also dividing the practitioner from his humanness, and while the spiritual work may be skillful, compassion for self (and for others) is inhibited, and the wounded ego goes unhealed.

These two situations can be changed through attending to the work of the South. It is never too late to start. The South offers resources of courage, vigor, enterprise, humor, and all manner of opportunities within relationship. What is asked for is your willingness to participate with honesty and integrity.

South teaches you about being yourself. It teaches you about alignment and alliance, and finding the ground that feels right to walk on. South lets the light shine as it will, letting go of fear about what will be seen. It is ongoing work, work that enriches rather than distracts from spiritual practice. At first it may feel like you are going backward as you open to the struggles of ego and are confronted by its excesses and deficiencies. It may offend your spiritual sensibilities. You may be tempted into denial.

Establish a perspective of compassion. As you peel away the beliefs layered over ego, applying discernment and using transcendent awareness as a reference to prevent constriction, you can find ways to honor your individuality without fixing your identity to it. You can find ways to operate in your practice that neither glorify nor deny self, but that include humanness in the divine connection.

two

ALLIANCE

Transformation is part of your engagement in each of the Directions. In the South transformation moves through interactions in the manifested matrix, that is, through relationship.

In *The Spirit of Place* there is much focus on spiritual alliance with the sacred beings of the Earth. One of the gifts of alliance is its transformative potential. This is realized through the experiences of becoming that with which you are allied, or of using that facility to transform self in other ways.

Within expanded consciousness you are able to resonate with all of the matrix, but your particle self is pitched to specific vibrations, which is why you feel special affinities to certain other beings in the matrix. These special connections are your totems and allies.

Resonance with your totems and allies is particularly strong and accessible. Those relationships can be vehicles of transformation. By aligning within resonance you can call upon attributes of the totem, or in effect become that totem to whatever degree is needed. This dissolves limiting self-beliefs as it expands your dimensions of identity and ability. You realize that self is more fluid than you thought.

This state of alignment with a totem can be used to bring about changes of many kinds. Because it suspends or alters your usual parameters, it allows you to instigate personality modifications, changes in the body, rearrangement of energy flows, disruption of mental formations, and release of emotional charges. The potentials of such actions for healing have made this use of totem relationship an enduring shamanic art.

Another means of transformation brought about through alliance can be found in the process of coming to terms with particular resonances. As you explore what underlies your association with certain totems and allies—that is, the nature of those resonances—you are faced with aspects of self that may or may not be easy to live with. A path of understanding and acceptance can lead to changes, or to a more Spirit-aligned embodiment and use of those aspects.

Shamanic relationships within the matrix put interaction into a sacred context, one that requires a basis of respect and multileveled perception. I have noticed that people often fall into limiting modes of relationship with totems and allies just as they do with humans. I categorize these modes directionally: East types of totem relationships tend toward the metaphorical, symbolic, and perpetually analyzed model. South relationships are experiential, kinesthetic, and linked strongly to personal identity. West relationships are empathetic, emotionally responsive, and sensitive to context. The North mode of totem relationship is task-oriented, operating on a practical level of cooperative purpose.

It may help to look at your totem alliances to see if you are making use of all the levels appropriate to those relationships. Because of habit or what you have been taught, it may not occur to you to investigate new perspectives of relationship. Expanding your work with totems deepens your connections and further integrates them into daily practices and experience.

It is a little strange to talk about spirits because there is not a consensus about what spirits are, where they dwell, or even if spirits exist. Different cultures, religions, and individuals have their own ideas about spirits and spirit realms. These reflect the vast array of views regarding the nature of reality and human experience. People working with spirits and spirit realms have their personal maps and ways of relating. In writing about invocation in part one, I referred to three of these modes: the dualistic, the metaphoric, and the particle/wave. The first and last of these are used by shamans; the second—

the metaphoric—is often present in shamanistic therapies.

Alliance is about connection and good relationship. Alliance with spirits extends connection into causative and supernatural stratas of reality. This is where you engage with or change the ordinary through the nonordinary. In this process you can also learn about yourself.

As a practitioner, if you are not learning about self through your spirit alliances, you are ignoring an aspect of your work in the South. On the other hand, if you use alliances exclusively as mirrors of self, you neglect the larger purpose of this gift and the larger reality of Self. Again, this comes back to the integration of particle and wave consciousness—the individual life aligned with wholeness.

Two personal illustrations of this South work around self and Self come to mind. Transcendent awareness came to me early in life, and ego work later; the sense of Self was often more real than the sense of self, and altered states were part of my idea of ordinary consciousness.

One autumn day my son brought me to visit a woman who has big cats and wolves living with her and her teenage son. We spent time bottle-feeding and playing with a frisky young African lion and a baby black leopard, then visited with a Siberian wolf. The huge wolf was very accepting of me. He leaned against my legs and gently held my hand in his mouth. This acceptance disarmed whatever fear I had, allowing love to freely flow both ways.

The bulk of our time was spent with the big cats—two mountain lions and an African lion who lived together in a fenced enclosure. The African lion was, of course, the largest of the cats, and the most sociable. He liked his tummy rubbed. He also liked to fix me with a terrifying, predatory stare, then rush at me as though to kill, swerving at the last moment. (Or sometimes a little past the last moment— he whopped me with his gigantic paw once, numbing my jaw for fifteen minutes. All in lion fun, naturally.) After I fed him the lion flopped down beside me in congenial companionship. He licked the food residue off my fingers, then took my whole hand into his cavernous mouth and gnawed it slightly, letting go instantly when he realized he had nicked my thumb. It was quite an experience having my hand in such a mouth.

The male cougar was more reticent. He watched from a distance, or brushed past me without eye contact. The cougar was lean and elegant beside the massive lion. The cougar seemed to want interaction but did not have the lion's genetic social arts. I did not push myself on him. As a solitary person, I recognized his dilemma.

The female cougar was more rambunctious. The instant I entered the enclosure she was on me, levitating from my feet to my shoulders, pushing lightly off my head and right shoulder as she bounded away. In a second she was back, leaping, knocking into me, everywhere at once. Her acrobatics were extraordinary—unnerving and intimidating. I found a wall to lean against and fended her off. Her coup-counting was the flip side of the male's uncertainty.

Though very rough, the female never became mean in her approaches. I collected my wits and met her challenges more firmly. At times it felt overwhelming to be with these three cats, their bodies in motion, their energies swirling around me. Their cat-ness was so intensely embodied, catalyzing my own cat-ness to an almost painful degree. There was a mutual yearning for contact despite the ingrained solitary natures we mirrored in each other.

The experience filled me in a way no human interaction does, and also was exhausting. I felt as though I had engaged in inner work that went so close to the core that all I could do afterward was curl up and sleep. The combination of exhilaration, longing, and peace that being with these cats stirred in me brought me in touch with parts of self that cannot be accessed transformatively with words or contemplation, or with other typically human approaches. The direct power of resonance with the cats, and with the wolf, brought change and healing within a context of encounter and relationship.

The second illustration concerning South work around ego involves cat-ness also. A woman who attended a sweat at our place called to say she had lost her wedding ring sometime during the ceremony. I had an immediate sense that it could be found, so went down to the lodge.

The sweat lodge was in a forest clearing. There were many standing and fallen trees, tangles of Oregon grape and salal, mosses and nettles. It was not an easy area to search for something so tiny. I asked the Panther totem to help—Cat spirits are adept at finding lost things, and at stalking in general. Vision shifted as consciousness aligned with the Panther medicine and I was quickly guided away from the lodge and into the surrounding forest.

I stopped among trees and brush, feeling it was the right spot, and began scanning the ground. The Panther spirit was very present. Despite my certainty, however, I could not find the ring. I sighed and gave up. "Some shaman you are," I grumbled to myself. Instantly I saw the ring, and laughed. When self completely lets go to Self, everything necessary is present. Even in altered states or in communion with the spirits, egotism can get in the way. When alignment fully dissolves boundaries there can be no interference from egotism—the particle and the wave become of one Mind and purpose.

three

Being Human

The plaintive cry "I'm only human" is often used as explanation for imperfect behavior, and humanness certainly seems to include frequent fallings short of what is considered ideal. At other times humans proudly proclaim our species the crown of creation, and humanness the epitome of divine reflection. This rather expansive niche we have claimed in the universe may or may not fit our true proportions. Over the centuries humanness has been defined in a variety of (sometimes contradictory) ways by scholars, philosophers, religious leaders, and scientists. (A notable feature of humanness seems to be an urge to articulate our distinction as a species.)

I have always had a sense of not being "only human," though being human seems fine. I think there is more to us than humanness, just as there is more to Self than ego. Humanness is a context of experience. Gender is a context too, perhaps a subcontext to humanness. People sometimes assume that I am uncomfortable with being a woman because I resist genderfying spirituality, or that I am an escapist from humanity because I include the rest of nature in Self.

Not so. My experience of Self's spaciousness and astounding potential makes it unnatural to confine Being to the smallness our society assigns genders or species. Every time I hear someone make a limiting statement about humans or other forms of being, I remember the exceptions I have encountered and realize how wonderfully elusive truth can be when we try to box it in. I hope we will always be free to be more than we (or others) think we are. That more-ness is part of how life evolves, how life participates in miracles as well as "ordinary" transformations. More-ness moves us out of ruts, out of conditioned thinking and belief and beyond defeatist resignation. It is part of greatness, part of transcendence, and part of love.

Assumptions about gender or species can close doors to expansive experiences. I have seen this happen many times, and seen how people benefit when they persist despite their assumptions. A Cheyenne sundancer attended a sweat lodge I conducted and had a strong experience in the ceremony. Afterward he confessed that he had had doubts about my ability to lead the sweat due to the fact that I am a woman, and he apologized.

A woman I chatted with prior to teaching a workshop looked at me in dismay when I stood up to begin the session, and blurted out, "You're the presenter?" At the end of the day she requested to be the sponsor for future workshops in her community. A married couple attending that same intensive became part of an ongoing group I regularly meet with for teachings. They recently confided that when they first came in the door and saw me they both thought, "She's too young."

It is not only assumptions about others that can impede movement, deprive you of vital lessons, and shadow your relationships. You can also pen yourself in with definitions that crowd your own wholeness. The way you live reflects inner images of self, and influences the formation of those images.

In our industrial, patriarchal society, children are brought up believing the tenets of consumerism and oppression, and are shaped (albeit not uniformly) by those destructive forces. Those who somehow confound that shaping become fringe-dwellers, radicals, or oddballs. Even subcurrents to the mainstream usually mimic negative characteristics of the dominant society, though the ways these manifest may be subtle.

This is not to say there is nothing worthwhile about modern society, but in its present form, at very best, it incompletely nourishes well-being. The self-images that arise in such an environment are malnourished versions of what a man or woman can be.

The manner in which we live in this society needs healing. Our world needs to become a place where children can grow into people of beauty and strength. I was fortunate to have parents who tried to raise their children in a nonsexist, nonracist, environmentally integrated way. I was never told that, because I was a girl, I could not do this or had to do that. My parents recycled and reused things. We were taught not to despise or maltreat other living beings. This made an impact on my life, on my beliefs about self and others, and on how I move in the world. It is likewise with my now-adult son, who was raised to see himself as whole and connected.

How we live as human beings is intrinsic to how we evolve spiritually. You cannot make war at home and make peace out in the world.

I was in the produce section of the grocery store one morning when an old man standing next to me began complaining about vegetables. "No rutabagas," he muttered. He looked sidelong at me as I poked at a package of tofu. "They got no rutabagas. They're a very sweet vegetable when they're fresh," he stated. "They got hardly any old kinds of vegetables here."

I agreed that the selection was sparse, and tried to continue my shopping. The old man stood there looking distraught. "Bet you don't even know what a rutabaga looks like," he challenged. "Young people [I am in my forties] don't know about those kinds of foods. It's all disappearing."

I struggled with my aversion to engaging with strangers, and let it be overridden by the need of this old man to be heard. I faced him fully and met his eyes. He drew himself up and proceeded to discourse on heirloom fruits and vegetables, and how they are becoming lost to us because no one cares, and young people are not learning about them.

He tried to list those foods for me—it was like an invocation. He faltered; his face strained. "I can't remember," he said, his voice shaking. "It's in my head but my tongue can't get it out."

There is so much disconnection in our society: age stratification, sexual division, racial separation, class hierarchy. Humanness is communal. How can our humanity be healthy without interrelationships that honor inclusiveness? The old man in the store was so unused to being heard that his brain seized up in the face of complete attention.

Lives battered by disrespect and violence can be healed by communion that listens, that touches in kind ways, that acknowledges common ground amid diversity. All the claims and debates about whether animals have group souls or no souls; about whether humans are the Earth's nervous system or genitals; about whether women are more sensitive or men more solar or Natives more wise matter not if we cannot transformatively address the foundations of how we live together.

To do this we need to focus not on distinctions but on what is shared. Basically everyone's needs are the same—to have clean air, water, and soil, and to feel respected and loved. What has happened that our world has moved so far from these foundations?

Instead of making self progressively smaller and smaller through definitions that diminish potential, why not expand the image of being, opening not only individual life to all manner of possibilities, but also reconnecting and nourishing the community of life as well? With reconnection comes common commitment to what serves the good of all. It may be awkward at first. We may stumble and lose focus, but of all the many things within our human capacity to do, this seems most worthy of our gifts.

I remember Stephen Levine describing the Dalai Lama as the most human person he had ever met. Spiritual evolvment is not dehumanization. If anything, if you include South work in that process, it brings you more deeply into humanness. Transcendent consciousness is not meant to be an escape from body or ego. Seeing or using it as such may be an indication that there are aspects of human experience with which you have unfinished business. It is pretentious to disdain embodiment, or to achieve detachment by closeting what chagrins you about self. The hallmark of spiritual maturity is the bringing of sacredness into the ordinary in a natural, graceful way. This is alignment, not severance of self. To be a conduit of divinity is to put all aspects of humanness at the service of love. Love refashions whatever has been disfigured by fear.

There are times when you may wish to be other than human—to be bird, or rainbow, or disembodied essence—and indeed these you can be, but not, in this life, to the exclusion of humanness. "Hey," I sometimes say to my dog, "don't be doleful—you're lucky to be a dog. You don't have to pay taxes or weep over the war in Bosnia." There is a purpose in what each of us is, and goodness to be found there. Being human is one of the pathways to wholeness, but there is no "only" about either the path or the condition.

four

Movement

The universe is characterized by movement. Life breathes in and out, hearts pulsate, light sings into being, the cosmos dances in a vast and intricate pattern of consciousness. The desire of life is to be and to become, and that desire invokes the contexts allowing expression.

As a gardener and witness in the wilderness, I see with constant awe life's desire unfolding in form, in beauty and vitality. The becoming-ness of plants and animals reaches into the light, unfurling leaf and wing, stretching muscles, uncoiling in the richness of Earthly context.

As a midwife I witnessed and helped human becoming-ness in its passage to this realm, seeing the other-world light shift in newborns' eyes as they opened to this stage in their journey.

There was one baby whose birth I attended who chose not to stay in this realm. Her body emerged from the womb with no vital signs—no heartbeat, no breath, no color. I saw her spirit hovering over the small, white form, and felt her resistance to taking it on. I urged her toward embodiment with my hands as I pumped her heart, and the other midwife gave her breath.

At the hospital she was mechanically and chemically sustained. Soon after the parents brought her home six weeks later, she died, asserting her choice once the body was released from interference. Sometimes being-ness does not move as we wish. Sometimes the mystery of the dance grieves us, and sometimes it helps us accept.

For a word to be heard there needs to be silence before and after. In the places we call stillness there is movement also—the pauses between inbreath and outbreath, the listening times, the quiet, the peace. Stillness could be thought of as receptive movement.

There are three primary ways I experience movement, and three ways I experience stillness. The first category of movement is that which is goal-oriented. The known purpose inspires and guides the action, whether that is walking across a room to get the car keys or bending a sapling into place for a sweat lodge.

The second kind of movement is oriented toward intuitive direction; an unknown but sensed purposefulness guides the doing. This may interrupt or preempt goal-oriented movement, or it may occur out of stillness. It is process-oriented: The bending of the sapling becomes an experiential focus in itself, regardless of outcome.

Habitual movement is the third category, and occupies an astounding percentage of all movement on the Earth. Instinctual action is included in this category, as are unconscious actions.

The ways of stillness are similar to the categories of movement. One kind of stillness is goal-oriented receptivity, present in some kinds of meditation or trance where priority of attention is purposeful. Goal-oriented receptivity can also be the sort of stillness that occurs when you are standing in the woods trying to hear a certain birdcall.

The second way of stillness is one that opens to the unknown. Again, this may take place in meditation or trance, or it may be present in more ordinary contexts. Alignment is to stillness itself, with trust that awareness will be drawn to the appropriate priority. Being in stillness is the focus.

The third kind of stillness is an abiding in peace—a stillness of true rest, whether in sleep or in waking consciousness. This is different from dull or lethargic states of inactivity. It nurtures all levels of being through a loving alignment with cosmic resource.

Stillness and movement can be effectively integrated as you mix and match these categories. Traditional disciplines such as Zen and Taoism focus on integration and refined application of movement and stillness, often with approaches that upend conventional concepts and assumptions.

Practices such as t'ai chi or other internal martial arts can teach you about your relationship to movement. I do t'ai chi in a variety of ways; each gives insights and amplifies different energy flows.

The first way I practice is very slow and attentive. In each moment I try to be aware of balances, shifts, and where the focus and flow of energy is. This is excellent practice for anyone doing hands-on healing work or other energy conducting. Through this observant manner of practicing t'ai chi, I have learned a great deal about movement habits and energy tendencies. It is a practice that facilitates rerouting of energetic flows and changes in habit. This can be important in creating a healthy, balanced vessel for energy to move through.

Sometimes it is difficult to discern these patterns in yourself, even if you are skilled at perceiving flows in others. Movement disciplines like t'ai chi or Feldenkrais make these patterns explicit. Observing yourself this way is also a practice in nonjudgment. In trying to "get it right" or in realizing that your grounding is poor or that you are having difficulty focusing energy and moving your body at the same time, you might encounter such "unenlightened" reactions as frustration or self-doubt. A precarious self-esteem may plummet.

This is a good point at which to remember that discernment will serve you better than judgment. Getting it right is not as important as paying attention to what and how you are learning. You can be an adept metaphysical practitioner and still make a beginner's raw mistakes as you explore movement of metaphysics through the physical.

Another way I use t'ai chi is in dance. This is traditionally frowned upon, but useful nonetheless. I either perform the actual form to music or incorporate movements from the form into spontaneous dance. Instead of meticulous, attentive focus, this practice centers on expressive movement. It shapes and releases feelings or held-in energies. It helps bring relaxation—loosening muscles, tuning up the body, and stabilizing emotions. It may assist in bridging ordinary and nonordinary realms by transferring energies from one to the other. The type of music used gives a certain pace, mood, and flow to what is done. This dance can be very deliberate or tuned entirely to what spontaneously arises.

The third way I use t'ai chi is more martial in expression. I either practice the form in a faster, more forceful manner, using breath and movement to cultivate and direct power; or I use elements of the form to clear unwanted energies from my space. I have an aikido practice sword, and use an eight-direction sword movement that is also effective for this. The martial work fosters strength and confidence. It encourages centering and responsibility for your actions, and teaches you to move with precision, clear intention, and specific impact.

The form of t'ai chi that led me to its practice is nonphysical. I began encountering an Oriental t'ai chi master sometimes when I was in trance. He never spoke but would demonstrate movements in slow motion, and the particular energy of the movements would visibly continue beyond his body, like ripples from a pebble dropped in a pond. Each gesture, each move had a distinctive continuance.

After recurring encounters with this master I asked my land partner to teach me the t'ai chi form. During those times when, due to circumstance or illness, I am physically unable to do the form, I enact it mentally or through an altered state. Sometimes I dream it. T'ai chi movements embody core patterns; many teachings lie within them.

The last way I use t'ai chi is for connecting with natural context. When the form is done in a grounded manner, it joins you with the natural energies around you. It can be a choreography of relationship—a giving and receiving of intimacy with the land and sky. In this practice you attune to connective energies—opening your being, weaving the filaments of terrestrial and celestial life force, participating in the sharing of light. It is a peaceful way to ask to know a place and to reveal your intentions of good relationship. This can be done in water also, a slow dance with a medium that is carrier and cleanser, mystery and nurturant womb-home.

T'ai chi movements put you in your feet, realizing the ground, the nourishment of condensed energy. They put you in your knees, teaching flexibility and intelligent action. They center you in your balance point, storehouse and intersection of vital forces. Their practice puts you in your hands, conductors and communicators of power and intention. And these movements bring you into your breath, primal connection to life and for life's sacred use.

Movement that aligns with wisdom and beauty is integral to any spiritual practice. As an embodied being, movement is a significant aspect of your experience. As a practitioner, attention to movement and stillness will give grounded dimension to knowledge. If you watch animals you will see how much of their medicine is expressed through the way they move. It is likewise for trees and plants in the patterns of their growth. These medicines can be brought into your own life and practice in both mundane and metaphysical ways.

Stones move also, but their clearest demonstration is of stillness. The teaching of stillness is patience; its gift is timelessness. The medicine of stillness is knowing. That is why people allied with stones, like Yuwipi medicine men, often have access to nonordinary avenues of knowledge.

Stillness—receptive movement—is often hard to come by for urban dwellers. The constant yet erratic energy of cities often creates agitation and overstimulation, leading to a numbing of attention. It is worthwhile to find times and places for stillness either within your usual context or in conducive retreats. Stillness is like the clarity of a rippleless pool; mountainlike, it feeds your endurance. It has the grace of those moments when the gusting wind ceases and the air is hung with birdsong. In stillness, spirit is heard.

five

Objects

In medicine work, objects can be used as physical tools to convey and facilitate the presence of spiritual power. They are not powerful in themselves, nor will they turn their possessors into powerful practitioners. In our society objects indicate position or financial achievement. In spiritual work it is more appropriate to take a utilitarian attitude toward objects, unless the traditional purpose of a given object is to usefully signify status or accomplishment.

There may be times in your practice when you use a large array of objects. It is important to attend to these objects appropriately. A common lapse for many practitioners is not maintaining objects properly. A medicine object—any object, really—is not just a generic form. There is a giveaway of life—of the Earth's resources—in the making of all things. This includes the resources used in manufacturing. Everything on this Earth comes out of the Earth, whether the end result is a plastic toy or a sacred carving in rare wood. In acquiring an object, this giveaway—or, more commonly, this long chain of giveaways—should be acknowledged and honored. The process of an object's making or availability should be considered. What mountain was desecrated by mining? what forest ravaged? what animals slaughtered? Most objects have taken shape through processes other than wise or respectful relationship with the land. Perhaps what is called for is reconsideration of how many objects you truly need. Perhaps there can be more active participation in the manufacturing or acquisition process, more questioning and responsibility, less consumerism.

Because objects come from life, they carry life energies and interact with what is around them. Medicine objects incorporate and emanate spiritual charges that are amplified by frequent, focused use and proper maintenance. Objects that are parts of natural beings—horns, claws, feathers, and so forth—can convey the medicine and serve as connectors to the spirits of those beings if the practitioner is in good relationship with the spirit.

Your interaction with objects is another South mirror of self. It may be beneficial to use this mirror in a way that leads to moderation in your use of objects. In asking yourself why an object attracts you, what your real needs are, what your best relationship with an object is, or how you are making use of objects, you may find that materialistic habits or ego issues have had insidious influences on your spiritual practice. Love of beauty, enjoyment of material forms, attraction to charged objects, and many other positive feelings can be expressed in your life through alternative means. You can appreciate and interact without having to acquire. I think my first lesson in this was when, as a child, my mother pointed out the respectful wisdom of admiring flowers without picking them.

Relationship to objects is directly reflective of relationship to the Earth and of attitudes and beliefs about life. When you walk a path that neither demeans nor demands objects, you move toward becoming happier in your life and more clear in your work.

Objects in your possession or ones that are brought to you may be charged with undesirable energies. Unless there is compelling reason to destroy them, these objects can and should be cleared and restored.

Elemental methods of clearing are usually effective: smudging, washing, purifying with light, or neutralizing with earth. When used with intent and skill, the elements generally are sufficient for eliminating programmed or inadvertent charges. If the charge is deeply enmeshed in the object's matrix, it will be necessary to repeat such clearings a number of times.

Before and during the clearing process, the object to be cleared should be kept wrapped or shielded and set apart from altars, personal space, or contact with anyone who may be affected by its influence. When working with the object, be sure to keep the surrounding area and yourself cleared also.

After clearing, instill either a blessing or, if you will be using the object, a positive charge. Elements such as sweetgrass, pure water, light, and crystals can be carriers for a blessing or a charge, or you can simply use prayerful focus.

When objects carrying exceedingly unpleasant or "hot" energies are brought to me I do not touch them directly until an initial clearing is completed. An intermediary tool can be used to lift or move these objects. I have learned to look carefully before I handle objects presented to me. Some people have no idea what it is they are carrying.

Learning the how-to's of clearing is basic to working with charged objects, but the how-to's are not where the work ends if you are seeking a more complete understanding in your practice. The most primary clearing must occur inside yourself, not in the object. If a troubled young person is given to your care, no amount of rehabilitation will clear the anxiousness and distress if you define the intrinsic reality of that person as troubled. Even if, in spite of your fixed perception, there is a change arising from the youth's own efforts, it will not seem real or will maybe not even be seen by you.

So it is with most objects. In order to clear something you must be able to see it *as itself*, to identify its essential nature as clear. If you cannot see this, your own beliefs and reactive emotions will continue to load the object and frustrate your attempts to free it. You must be able to differentiate between influence and being.

This is usually easier to do with objects other than your own. Things that carry personal connotations, such as memories of intense relationship, hurts, grief, or neediness, or objects whose use was long-term, are far more challenging to clear because of what the sight of them evokes.

The first response to address in clearing any object is fear.

Acknowledge and dispel (or at least calm) any fear that is present before you work with an object. Otherwise you may invite harm.

Second, sense what charge the object carries. Keep grounded within your strength as you do this. Investigate the charge without being drawn into its field of influence. What you want is an idea of what is present, not an immersion in it. Be sure to note your first impression—this is usually the most accurate one.

Third, if the object is your own, consider your relationship with it. Survey your feelings and associated images. Get a sense of whether you are prepared to accept this object's continued presence in your life or whether it needs to go elsewhere instead. If the object belongs to someone else, ask what associations they carry regarding it—what feelings, thoughts, experiences. Either way, do this after your initial scanning, not before.

All the associations and energies an object carries intertwine to create your complexity of reactions to and beliefs about the object. The complexifying can give a process for understanding; the unraveling of energies can bring you a wider perspective of the healing needed beyond the clearing of the object. With this perspective it often becomes apparent what needs to be done, not only with the object but also within self.

Finally, go back to your first impression of the object's charge. Focus on your breath, empty your mind, and check the object again, verifying, modifying, or adding to your initial impression. When you began this encounter, you may or may not have been able to see beneath the influences affecting the object's energy field. Regardless, now is the time to perceive and address the essential nature of the object, to see it as clear and to reflect that back to the object as a mirror of true being.

This kind of seeing invokes love as well as clarity, and so restores good relationship. Maintain this as you dispel or transform the influences overlaying or woven into the object's matrix. Speak to the forces guiding the object's function, affirming integrity. Take responsibility for whatever you have projected into that object, and release the unhealthy aspects of that bond.

If the object is someone else's, pray for right relationship to awaken as you clear whatever is appropriate for you to intervene with. Intervention is first of all a matter of permission from that object's caretaker, but is also an arena for wisdom, competency, and guidance. Simple clearing is one thing, best taught to the person to whom an object belongs. Dealing with loaded charges is something else altogether. The former is housekeeping; the latter is a process of disarming.

It helps to look back to the circumstances under which an object originally came to you (or to the person to whom the object belongs). Examining those circumstances and the forces at play in them—the reasons and feelings behind something being purchased or given or the context in which something was found—gives clues to what that object carries and to its role in your relationship with it. This may be the context to which you restore the object, either in reclaiming those energies in your relationship with it or in physically giving the object back to that context.

Fearfully or bitterly destroying an object will not change its reso-nant energies within you. Those will perpetuate through some other focus. Giving an object to the elements can be an aspect of a releas-ing or clearing process, but it must be done with love and respect or the negativity with which this act is performed will rebound. The charges held in objects are representative of currents moving through relationship. Aberrant charges are the symptoms, not the sources, of ill.

There are times when it is wise to rid yourself of objects, or to ask help in dealing with them when you find their influences to be over-whelming. In the desire to reclaim something that once brought hap-piness or to not be defeated by shadows, you do not want to ignore your immediate needs relative to well-being.

I have found that it is difficult for an object to become ill-charged if the original circumstances of its coming to you and your original relationship with it were good and full of clear intention. Later pro-jections that are unfavorable tend to overlay, rather than become entangled with, the object's essential matrix. Thus they are fairly easy to clear. Ambiguous feelings about an object make that object more susceptible to an ill-wisher's manipulation of its charges. Fear leaves the door open for whomever or whatever would seek to harm.

Immediately when I moved to the mountain I now live on, I began having intense encounters with huge rattlesnakes. These experiences were not ordinary or coincidental. As I struggled to find a right path with the medicine of these snakes, I tried assiduously to avoid invoking them.

One day a visitor's truck ran over a small rattler on the driveway. When I found the dead snake, I made prayers and put it in the brush with some tobacco. A few weeks later I felt I should return to that snake and take its bones to work with in order to facilitate coming to terms with rattlesnake medicine. The snake was easily found, its bones nearly stripped by the small beings of the ground. I picked it up, and in doing so caused its rattles to shake, a sound which admittedly made me jump in alarm. Then I laughed at myself.

I took the bones home and sat outside with them, carefully and with great fascination separating the remaining dried skin from the linked vertebrae. I prayed aloud continuously as I cleaned and smudged the bones, speaking earnestly to the snake, to Rattlesnake, to the viper medicine in myself, and to the mountain the snakes and I both live on. I put the vertebrae and skull, and the rattles, fangs, and some of the skin, into an octagonal jar with some sage, sweetgrass, and tobacco. Finally, I took the jar into the house, into my room, and then thought a long time about where to put it. This was no small matter.

I put the jar on the windowsill beside my bed, then looked at the snake inside. It was too much. I found a beautiful red, gold, and black cloth—part of a tobacco offering given me—and wrapped the jar in this, tying it with a black ribbon. I set a sprig of mountain lichen on top. It seemed better now.

Each evening I spoke to Snake, even if just to bid it goodnight. I smudged the jar frequently. Since then my relationship with the rattlers, and with self, has changed. We are blessed to be in a universe that offers so many levels in which to enact the work that helps us grow and find peace.

six

PERSONAL RELATIONSHIPS

Some metaphysical practitioners draw distinct boundaries between their personal and professional relationships, and some do not. This may partly depend on the type of work a practitioner does or on the type of people she works with. Since natural spirituality is about integration, you might suppose this would apply to the continuum of personal/professional relationships as well, but the matter is not so simple.

When you separate the personal from the professional, it is easy for a divided persona to emerge along with divided relationships. You may begin to be one person for your clients or students and another for friends and family. Image-making can arise, inevitably followed by inner conflict or some other response to this level of dishonesty about self. Image-making necessitates keeping up fronts, and if you are adept at it, you will even fool yourself after a while.

An undivided you is someone recognizable to both clients and your family and close friends, no matter the context of encounter. While it may be necessary for you to acknowledge a degree of difference between personal and professional self in terms of priorities about what is being expressed, this is not the same as dividing yourself or creating an image of yourself. This is knowing what is appropriate to various situations. A trance session is probably not the time to chatter about your daughter's success on the basketball court, for example.

There are exceptions to this in work involving transcendent states of being. The Hopi dancers personifying kachinas *are* kachinas during those ceremonies. In that context self submerges in Self—ego is not a significant player. This also happens with totem medicine work and with shamanic possession. (Channeling will be discussed in a later chapter). With this sort of work there is a useful demarcation between the personified spirit's presence and the return of ordinary egoic self.

There was a period of time in my work with the sweat lodge when I found myself merging with several old-time Native medicine people while I was leading the ceremony. Usually their presences would come and go unobtrusively during the ceremony, though something of them lingered afterward. On one occasion I exited the lodge after everyone else had gone out, and when I emerged and saw the people sitting around the fire, they all looked totally foreign to me. "Who are all these white folks, and what are they doing here?" I wondered, with some degree of bewildered irritation. I did not know a single one of them, though one was my husband and another my best friend.

My demeanor was so changed that people later told me they knew something else was present, and were a bit intimidated but accepting. As I stood there, the shift began that returned me to ego consciousness. The moments between were particularly strange, realizing that I knew these people but still was not sure who they were.

When you are in the conductor's role during ceremonial work, even if you are not personifying the Goddess or a kachina or a totem, you have to clearly align self with Self so that ego does not assume a dominant position in consciousness. Alignment is always the most essential preparation of personal and professional selves. When there is integrity, people respect and trust your work in a leadership role. People who know you personally will then have no conflict about accepting you professionally.

The converse of this is when people support you in your professional role despite your dubious personal life, because it sheds some luster on them to be associated with you. This has little to do with friendship or integrity and much to do with neediness and egotism. Integrity—consistency of alignment—expresses itself in whatever way is appropriate to specific situations, whether personal or professional. It is a presence of the sacred in both ordinary and extraordinary contexts—the constant reference of self to core truths.

This does not preclude foibles and imperfections or mistakes. Image-making is fear based. This can be seen in practitioners who worry that the things they are good at will be discounted if people peek behind the facade hiding what the practitioner is not yet good at, or at what makes the practitioner just another human being. In a society that fawns on, and then ravages, its celebrities and heroes, this fear—and the barriers around self that result—are easily stimulated. In the spiritual community especially, great care is taken to obscure discrepancies between the shining professional self and the tarnished personal self. Illusion and judgment are partners here, going round and round as practitioners barter truths for image.

As a practitioner, you can best be both a human being and a divine conduit when you stop separating the two, and at the same time take responsibility for being not only honest regarding your humanity but committed to spiritual alignment.

Another arena for integrating personal and professional self is in your relationship with friends. If friends avoid your ceremonies or workshops, or skirt around your metaphysical skills when it would seem natural for them to ask your help, you may want to take a closer look at these relationships. Does your personal conduct make these friends leery of your professional activities? Are there issues of envy or competitiveness infiltrating these relationships? Are there unspoken conflicts that need airing? Are your friends afraid you will no longer treat them as peers if they become students, clients, or participants in ceremonies you lead? Are they afraid of becoming vulnerable or of not being respected if they confide in you as a practitioner? Are they concerned about lack of reciprocity? money issues? confidentiality? Are they unwilling to see you as an adept? Has friendship kept pace with personal change and growth?

Look closely at your participation in these relationships, and the way you treat your clients or the people you teach or help through ceremony. Are you doing things that justify your friends' avoidance? When friends prefer to engage with you on a personal basis only, it may simply be that your spiritual work is at variance with their own beliefs or that they are just not interested in it. These friendships may still be rich and enduring. When friends do choose to engage with you as a practitioner, it is important to honor the particular gift of that dimension of relationship. As the above questions indicate, there can be many issues that block this dimension from ever being explored. To have the people who best know your ups and downs— your humanness and struggles—support and value your use of spiritual gifts is a great affirmation and display of trust.

In your work with friends or family, be sure to keep ego in its right place, and remember that being the "expert" in one facet of relationship does not invest you with overall authority or indicate higher evolvement. Do not neglect other aspects of your friendship—the fun, sharing, and mutual respect. Be aware of how much "expertise" someone really wants—do not become pedantic.

In apparent contrast to friends who avoid your services are friends who take it for granted that you are at their disposal without giving consideration to how such help should be asked for. This can include bypassing meaningful protocols, assuming that they should receive for free that which others pay for, or ignoring what goes into the work you do, such as by giving no thought to the preparations and consequences associated with performing spiritual mediation on their behalf. These relationships may carry the same undercurrents as those with friends who avoid your work, and can be examined through some of the same inner questioning.

Added to these may be a mirroring of your own ambiguities about self-worth, the value of your work, and the basis on which that work is offered. Clearing the ambiguities can directly change your way of responding to exploitative relationships and to people's perceptions of your work.

The integration of personal and professional selves can invite ongoing pressure from people you help or teach who want to become your friends. The less professional your persona, the more this occurs. Some of this is due to how intimately you see those you do healing, counseling, or deep teaching with. Some of it is a mistaking of Spirit for the human being through whom Spirit moves.

I found this same phenomenon in my practice of midwifery. There is a level of bonding, a necessary trust, that is a natural aspect of the work, and people often seek to express and perpetuate this through friendship. Some clients or students have a need to bring the relationship into an arena where they can feel equal. It does not seem to occur to them that practitioners engage with hundreds of people on a basis of intimacy, and that it is not possible or desirable to translate all of these relationships into personal friendships.

There are times when someone you meet during occasions of teaching or healing will resonate with you in ways that open into friendship. In cases where this includes sexuality or romantic love, the practitioner must consider and act within what is professionally and personally ethical. These situations demand clarity and integrity.

Powerful spiritual practitioners will always attract sexual or romantic interest, as well as interest in friendship. The energies involved and the nature of the work stirs that attraction. Abuse in the area of sexuality and personal relationship is not rare in the shamanic and metaphysical communities. It is part of unresolved egotism and unhealed connections between men and women. Such abuse shadows the trust and intimacy natural to spiritual work and good relations and brutally exploits the yearning people have for spiritual knowledge, union, and acceptance.

The integration of personal and practitioner selves is not a simple achievement. It is something every person dances with in his or her own way, learning as they go. Discussion with teachers and other practitioners can aid reflection on these issues. These need to be brought into the open—not to condemn individuals or to push blame around in circles, but with intention to heal our relationships. As practitioners we need to be trustworthy, and as humans we need to help each other align with the integrity that can properly carry that responsibility.

seven

SOLITUDE

Some people are alone wherever they are and in the company of whomever they are with. That is one kind of solitude. This chapter will touch on the solitude of being without human company.

I sit in the deep silence of a winter night. The mountain is awake. The depth of silence is a presence that surrounds. Sometimes I feel the house is within the weighted core of the mountain; sometimes drifting like a boat in the moonless, starry sky. Having no electricity, I write by candlelight. The only sound is the fire in the woodstove— the warm soul of the house so contained in this cold, forested night. The candle flames are steady, like my thoughts. The cats watch the moving pen as though hypnotized. The dog sleeps beneath the stove, more soundly than cats ever do.

Solitude. I have often had it, scarcely interrupted, week upon week: the snowfall, sometimes exquisite, sometimes maddening in its serenity; and the nights that begin in afternoon, eclipsing the day as my inner shadows sometimes darken the light of equanimity.

"You must miss your son," the guy delivering firewood in October said, "and not having someone to bounce things off of." While I never picture my "things" as especially bouncy, it was a good point. Alone, you don't get important feedback from your species about your perspectives.

There are no safety nets in solitude, no runaway truck lanes. The longer you are alone, the more difficult it becomes to reenter into companionship. There have been times when I have hidden like a skittish animal at human approach, or have felt overwhelmed at entering a supermarket after a stretch of time in the wilderness. In solitude, in the wilds, your aura extends. Sensitivity is not abused; you can let go of psychic filters. After such a time away from society, you are not prepared for the barrage to your senses when you return. Being in the wilderness, you forget your social skills. You are not sure you are communicating appropriately when the clerk makes small talk. You have forgotten how to make small talk.

The smell of diesel, the blare of construction, the aisles and shelves and stacks of senseless merchandise, the intensity of electric lights, the faces of bored and bitter despair—you have forgotten all these. Your aura flattens, your senses contract, your mind tries to backtrack: Was the world always this crazy? Am I crazy? It feels like something is crazy. The urge to retreat again tugs on you like a friend trying to pull you out of the path of an oncoming train.

Social acclimation after solitude can be trying. It helps to move slowly and kindly, and to be among quiet and understanding people. You may feel like an alien or a newborn; you may feel raw and buffer-less. You may feel unreasonably fragile, or be experienced by others as uncomfortably observant, or too silent. Nuances seem like blatancies.

Sensitivity is heightened in solitude. Nature does not engage in emotional games—you become accustomed to truth from your environment.

Assuming you have a choice, what is the point of solitude? Why seek it? Humans are communal—why subject yourself to what is bound to make you a bit weird? Unless you are a hermit who is into austerities or miraculous meditation feats, why do it?

When choosing solitude as a counterpoint to your usual daily life, the less distraction you have the better. Without distractions or busywork, you at some point bump into yourself. This encounter may precipitate agitation, self-confrontation, or fear, especially if you have successfully avoided yourself for a long time. If self is familiar but disliked, you may end up depressed, feeling stuck and hopeless with what seems to be an immutable identity.

The hazard in engaging in long periods of solitude is a loss or skewing of perspective. The agitation or depression can become excessive and unchecked. Eccentricity can wobble into full-scale spinout. If you carry the potential for these into solitude, you must also bring along some resources for dealing with them. There is little sense in trying to avoid yourself—if you truly seek avoidance, start with avoiding solitude.

The resources that help one spend useful time alone are tools of consciousness. Meditation is one, particularly observation meditation. Another is the capacity to be still and to be peaceful in that stillness. An often unmentioned ace in the hole is a sense of humor about yourself. This has saved me countless times. Humor is a reliable perspective-shifter.

Applying discernment instead of judgment is essential, as is the ability to connect with and draw assistance from your natural surroundings. When outlook closes in you need to be able to expand perspective. Spirit allies may be present, but if you are emotionally shut down you may not be receptive to them.

The habitat around you can help equilibrium return. Use elemental therapy. If you are feeling spaced-out, spend time with big stones or dig in the dirt. If you are stuck in mental chatter, sit beside a waterfall. If you are despondent and weepy, climb a hill and let the wind blow over you. Hug a tree, burn prayer ties in a fire, take a walk, watch clouds, smudge yourself. There are many ways to shift your emotional state and come back to center.

The absense of human company gives unique opportunities to develop relationships with other forms of life and to experience being the minority species in your environment. This is one of solitude's most necessary gifts. When even one other human is present, your experience of nature is changed.

Spending time alone in the wilds brings the magic of deepening perception. Awareness tunes to subtleties of sound, light, fragrance, texture, detail. Attention is rewarded by experiential knowledge that is all the more meaningful for its direct transmission. You begin distinguishing shadings of tone in the spectrum of what meets the senses: the many caresses of moving air, the gradations of color in a leaf, the differences in the songs of two birds of the same kind. These teachings yield not only greater understanding (and survival knowledge), but deeper wonder and respect. They awaken instinctive wisdom as your connectedness within the web is called into active participation. You become a natural human being.

An intrinsic aspect of humanness, and our purpose within embodiment, is communal. But the perceptiveness, sensitivity, awakened awareness of connection, and quiet mind that solitude can engender are essential contributions to human community as well as to self. Until we learn to be natural humans, part of a larger communalism on Earth, we will be at odds with ourselves and our relations.

Prayer can be one of your resources during times alone. In solitude you can freely pray aloud—it may be the only talking you do. When you are abiding in more silence than you are used to, spoken prayers carry unusual power and significance. You speak and hear them in a more conscious and impressionable way.

When embarking on a period of solitude, you may have specific goals, such as total silence, extensive meditation, or communion with nature, or you may just want to have some time alone. Whatever the case, unless you have already made your peace, you will have to come to terms with self's presence.

People who are the most comfortable with solitude are often those who are very sensitive to the needs, moods, and feelings of others. For them, solitude is a great relief. Those most uncomfortable with being alone are usually those who use others as their reference for existence. Solitude for them can be terrifying, or unbearably boring.

Those who live in solitude develop techniques for maintaining mental balance, though a certain degree of eccentricity seems inevitable. Some people listen to the radio to include human voices and the human world in their habitats. Others establish a regular routine of activity to move them through their days and keep them from bogging down. Most find themselves talking aloud to themselves or to companion animals.

The most important facet of productively using solitude for inner work, whether during short-term retreat or long-term lifestyle, is the capacity to return again and again to your core alignment. If you can do this, you can move through fear, depression, and loss of perspective. You can dare the depths of self if you can always find your way back to that alignment to your truth.

What helps me most in this is threefold: prayer, awareness of beauty, and remembering that I am loved. The thread that joins the three is gratitude. Life is a grace. Sometimes, in solitude, the recognition of that is very clear. Aloneness takes things down to the bone, teaching you what is important and what is not. It can help you develop self-discipline, resourcefulness, intelligent pacing of energy, creativity, mindfulness, ingenuity, spiritual stamina, and simple enjoyment. But aloneness itself is not enough. Within it must be cultivated both purposeful momentum and a quality of stillness and patience.

The mountain night seems vast and secret. The frost of its breath rimes the evergreen needles. The bears are dreaming in the mountain's pockets, dreaming the spring as cubs gestate within bears and bears within season.

Solitude's time is measured but unnumbered. It moves with the light, with each embrace of dawn, with unmooring into night. In solitude the star's music is faint but there. How many times have I watched the moon moving, the stars moving, between silhouetted branches, the seated bulk of mountains?

In silence the feel of things startles; there is an acuteness of fingertips and skin. The light is poignant on tree bark and rock, all colors precious to the gathering gaze. I harvest daylight, naming it for memory: ravens in the pearl-trunked aspens; coyote running low as I labor up the trail; two bald eagles black as the ravens, white as the snow, sailing on the afternoon quiet without a wing beat.

In solitude I face my worst critic. I have ample time for regrets, ample time for panic about prospects, no one to jolly me out of it or give reassurance or point out other options.

When I was twenty I lived alone for some weeks in an adobe hut on a mountain in Spain. There was no road—my transport was a grumpy donkey named Antonio who shared my hut and would give a shattering bray in the middle of the night in protest of bats.

In this solitude I spent hours sitting in the doorway watching ants and smoking hash, and had a hard time adjusting to humanity when I ventured back to the world of people. Sometimes I wonder if I have changed much—other than giving up hash and becoming less fearful of the dark—but the teachings of solitude include acceptance. The change that matters is the patiently unfolding compassion that has its roots in making peace with self, and has its fruits in the capacity to take solitude's gifts of beauty and clarity forth into the world.

Walking from field into forest,
twilight's temple, there are unfinished
sentences to this day.
Now evening, first stars unveiled,
scraps of clouds passing eastward
backtracking the day.
Clouds and walking,
the gestures that trail the half-speech
of yearning, the life unbuilt,
the prayer caught on grief's thorn.
Into the winter forest
each tree is stilled
in its last thought of autumn,
all other memories given to the dreaming Earth.
I hear nothing
but my own footsteps
in this afterhours gallery, sacred
in its integrity and its mystery,
evening star poised above the hill
and trees waiting
for its light like pilgrims at their destination.
I walk upon stillness
and sit a while
until the cold becomes a grace.

PART THREE

West
Water

one

Love

West work on the medicine wheel deepens awareness of the heart. Whatever your path and practice, it must center in the heart if it is to bring you to wholeness.

The heart is where sacred reality is magnetized into expression. Instead of basing your path on what you are against, the heart remembers what you are for. It is your place of goodwill.

A friend once told me that there are only two basic emanations: love and fear. All else derives from these. In natural spirituality you look for primality in things, for core places in which to focus your transformative work. Instead of struggling with symptoms such as anger, anxiety, and jealousy, you look to the generative basis of these feelings, which is fear. Instead of casting about for some positive attitude to don, you ground your alignment in the source of spiritual nourishment, which is love.

Whenever you are faced with choices of action or response, you can use a core reference question: Will this choice serve love or fear? The asking itself interrupts habitual patterns. This causes acute discomfort at times, a wrenching away from conditioning, a tripping-up of emotional momentum. It may feel so righteous to go ahead with anger. It may feel impossible not to be fearful. Intense encounters may overwhelm or make you forget your commitment to love. Situations may move so fast and choices be so reflexive that you blink past awareness of other options.

When this happens, you can still take time afterward for honest reflection (not self-judgment). Do not be ashamed of fearfulness, but also do not defend it—either of these reinforces its grasp. Fear constricts perception, making options difficult to ascertain. Love expands possibility, bringing to light previously unseen resources. In surveying options ask yourself: How can love be made manifest in this situation? Each manifestation of love strengthens its reality in world consciousness. *It is the place of greatest power in your life, the choosing of love or fear.*

When we are divided from each other we suffer. A person feeling separation because of gender, race, class, age, ability, and so forth, suffers. In separation they feel others cannot really know their suffering, cannot really understand how their pain feels. Whole segments of society dwell in this feeling of separation and suffering.

The only healing is true connectedness. How do we connect? Through compassion, an attribute of love. Compassion is a higher octave of empathy. When you are empathetic, you are sensitive to other's feelings. Empathy may open into connectedness, but it often ends up amplifying or multiplying suffering: instead of one person feeling bad, two people do.

It may also be complicated by the need of the emphathizer for there to be satisfactory resolution of feelings so that their own discomfort is relieved—a "be happy so I can be happy" attitude. Empathy can as easily lead to resentment as to love. An empathetic person often feels a strong need to be alone, or to make relationships with people who keep their auras to themselves.

Sometimes empathy follows from unclear perceptions. A response to someone's feelings may be to project erroneous interpretations of those feelings or of their causes. These misunderstandings exacerbate separation instead of dissolving it.

Compassion, on the other hand, is acceptance. When compassion is present, perception does not trigger the need for a certain outcome. What is experienced is connectedness itself—not just to others but, more usefully, to love. This enables you to be sensitive without becoming enmeshed in whatever the feelings are, including your own. When suffering is met with compassion, it encounters the healing power of love. Instead of the drain on well-being that empathy can spur, compassion gives strength. Compassion removes separation, exposing pain to love.

On the medicine wheel, West is the place of the adult or parent, as East is the Direction of the child and South the place of the youth. The youth is involved with individuality and warrior stuff—honor, bravery, action, pride, confrontation. The parent's perspective moves to what is needed for love to be experienced. The parent is concerned with healing, with caring, with letting go of me-ness so that change can be facilitated: this is the mother who gives up sleep to nurse a baby, or who sets her work aside to listen to a child's news. The letting go and giving allow what is tender and fresh to grow and be nurtured.

In the West this fluidity of letting go and shifting focus is applied to beliefs and to states of consciousness, as well as to relationships. Instead of saying "I'm right, this is me, this is my space, these are my needs and my boundaries," it expresses willingness to dissolve boundaries in order for there to be change, movement, growth, transformation, healing, acceptance. It is the process in which the cocooned caterpillar liquefies itself, restructuring identity and form in acceptance of metamorphosis.

Part of the willingness to participate in change is the willingness to forgive, another attribute of love. Forgiveness is often misunderstood as condoning wrongdoing or setting yourself up as a sucker. Forgiveness of self is sometimes similarly misunderstood as indulgently letting yourself get away with wrongdoing, of not facing up to and being accountable for personal behavior.

These concepts have nothing to do with forgiveness, which is a recognition and acceptance that makes room for healing. To be unforgiving is to cling to hurt out of fear. The fear may be that the perpetrator of your hurt will go unpunished, or that forgiveness will be a forgetting or an encouragement, leaving you open to experiences that hurt again.

Forgiveness does not trivialize pain, invite recurrence, or condone evil. Forgiveness allows you to move through and out of suffering, and to recognize its multi-causative nature. It encourages discernment instead of judgment. Forgiveness enables you to extract whatever teachings are offered by a situation, and it releases the harmful energies binding you or others to wrongness. For these reasons, forgiveness makes repetition less, instead of more, likely to occur.

I used to think forgiveness was not my responsibility. "Let God forgive," I would mutter. "Who am I to mess in such matters?" I have since come to see forgiveness as a blessed aspect of the human job description; now it is judgment, grudge-holding, and hoarded suffering that I would just as soon not be occupied with. Forgiveness puts you in the now, accessible to well-being.

A related and similarly confusing subject is trust. Both trusting and forgiving are often equated with being naive or gullible. Trust, faith, and belief are muddled in our conversations. I visualize faith as a rock, belief as the compound faith and other mental structures are made of, and trust as a condition of relationship. To trust is to place confidence in something's tendency to act according to its nature.

Following this definition, it plainly benefits you to have an accurate perception of that thing's nature. If I trust my cat to not lick the butter dish that sits on the counter I will probably be disappointed, because it is this cat's nature to lick butter dishes. If I have faith in his not licking it, I may or may not be disappointed; it depends how solid and well constructed the rock of my faith is. It may be strong enough to influence the nature of the cat or the reality in the kitchen. But unlike trust, faith cannot be betrayed, only tested—an interesting difference.

The more you understand the nature of something, the more sure is the ground upon which your trust rests and the clearer is the relationship between you. Understanding is a process that implies a level of connection. When connection exists in a larger realm of potential, trust can then allow for change, as well as reliability, in inherent nature. That kind of trust is not a precarious burden on the trusted or an unrealistic expectation from the entruster. For example, within the larger realm of potential I do not define my cat by his propensities.

Rather, I recognize his capacity to express his nature in ways that are harmonious with good relationship. Through that recognition I remove limitations imposed by a paradigm of separate interests.

Acceptance is the theme joining compassion, forgiveness, and trust. Each of those attributes of love catalyzes transformation through acceptance. The fear that compassion, forgiveness, or trust will be betrayed comes from misunderstanding how these servants of love function and how acceptance helps things move instead of stagnate. Fear is particle self's perspective, a me-them opposition that the West's more fluid, heart-centered perspective expands into mutuality.

People lament frequent betrayals of trust and openness, wondering how to abide simultaneously in trust and vigilance. They become cynical, suspicious, or guarded. One solution is to shift from vigilance to attention, as the first is oriented to particle self and the second to particle within wave. Attention can inform you of a situation's nature and the energies at work therein. It allows you to participate wisely.

Openness in itself is only appropriate when you are centered in loving attention. If not, it is to love that opening first needs to be made. The West shows you how to get unstuck; how to flow, be flexible, make adjustments, adapt, evolve; how to move in the river, with the river, as the river. Orientation to love allows fluidity in your responses to situations. It relieves the compulsion to take a stance and instead provides a basis for instinctually appropriate response.

A magician named Axis described four choices of ways to move in relation to the heart's desires: fulfillment, transcendence, modification, or abidance. Each of these calls on different capacities; with each of these choices are lessons about perception, belief, will, and wisdom. Whatever way is chosen to realize desire's intentions in any given situation, the core reference needing to be made is to love.

two

ALTERED STATES

Using the particle/wave model of consciousness orientation, altered states are those in which particle-self awareness moves into expanded consciousness. This can be a particle-with-particle awareness (shamanically being-with), a resonant integration of particles (being another particle, or within its awareness), a particle-within-wave consciousness (simultaneous personal and transcendent awareness), or a completely wave-oriented consciousness (cosmic awareness). Most meditative or shamanic trance states fall into one or more of these variations.

Visualization can be called upon in an altered state but is not itself an altered state. It is a tool of both ordinary and nonordinary consciousness. Visionary states, on the other hand, are usually of the particle-within-wave category. (Within the definition of *particle* I include both specific nonhuman or discarnate entities as well as egoic consciousness within the manifested matrix. I use the word *particle* to mean identifiable, specific expressions of consciousness.) Encounters with deitific forces can also be part of visionary experience. Transcendent awareness opens to whatever contexts or forms convey the necessary understandings or transmit the necessary energies.

When you work frequently with altered states you tend to become sensitized to your particular induction vehicles. The sound of drumming or bells, a whiff of a certain incense, the sight of a psilocybin mushroom, or the assumption of a particular posture might spontaneously trigger shifts in consciousness. Once pathways to altered states of consciousness are conditioned to certain threshold mechanisms, the states may be easily accessed. Over the years this may evolve into induction that is deliberately set in motion using only a mental image of the vehicle, or no vehicle at all.

Another simplification that might emerge over time, if you do not get immersed in performance and paraphernalia, is less reliance on objects and ritual. Many practitioners use these mainly for the sake of others, not for their own focus and movement in subtle realms. A naturopathic physician I apprenticed with used a pendulum to dowse remedies for his patients. He also used it for past-life and aura work in his practice. He confided that, after some years, he ceased needing the physical pendulum for these things—he could easily use his finger as a pendulum, or tune his whole awareness to receive the information he was seeking—but his patients related more comfortably to his use of the object.

Ceremonial performance and ceremonial objects can be beautiful, powerful to experience, and useful, and certainly there is enduring place for them. The point I make here is that when personal work reaches a level of transcendent attunement, ceremonial forms and objects become expressions of expanded consciousness, not paths to that expansion. Like people, objects and forms are better loved when neediness is not the driving force in relationship.

Sometimes people experience a sort of contact high from being around someone who is in an altered state. It is true that one person's expanded level of consciousness can change the level around them. This is one of the advantages of coordinated events like the harmonic convergence or the annual new year's peace meditation. Group meditations can be beneficial in general, even if the group is only comprised of two people. Covens, spiritual gatherings, ceremonial events, and churches all operate on a basis of people coming together to create a spiritual focus that is more than the sum of its parts.

What are some features of an altered state? It transcends time, space, physical dimension, individuality, and other ordinary boundaries. It transforms beliefs, conditions, and alignments. It is revelatory, and connects you to Self (or something beyond).

Individuals interpret the experience of these features according to what they believe from practice or what they have been taught. A Core shamanic practitioner may talk about the upper, middle, and lower worlds of spirit, and about power animals. A Christian mystic may refer to heaven and hell, angels and God. A Buddhist adept may move through mandalic abodes, or refer to bardos and other such realms. Different realms may be accessed by different practitioners, or the same realms may be accessed with differing perspectives. Two competent healers may not perceive someone's aura the same way.

If you are hoping for consistency of interpretation, you will be frustrated by all this. What is consistent about altered states are their characteristic features, not their interpretive applications. Looking beneath idiosyncratic terminology you will find common universal threads woven by religious, cultural, or individual contexts into interpretive models. The basic look and feel of altered states, however, is the same the world over.

Imagination works differently from nonordinary consciousness. It reflects rather than reveals. Creative imagination can be inspired by expanded consciousness, tapping into that potential and translating its flow into a stream of personal thoughts, feelings, or impressions. But imagination does not have the integrity of visionary experience, which when it occurs is uninterrupted and cohesive. Imagination does not transmit transcendent wisdom or power, or take you beyond egoic consciousness.

Some of the most distinct memories you may carry are those from moments that opened you into some kind of larger overlay. For example, I remember a time when I was cross-country skiing with my mother. I was about eleven years old. I recall following behind her, staying in her ski tracks, and becoming tired, cold, and uncomfortable with the unfamiliar and strenuous movements of this activity. The snow seemed adversarial and my mother unsympathetic. I fixed my eyes on the back of her boots and fell into a hypnotic state where distances passed unnoticed. Today when I recall that memory I can still see those boots moving in front of me, and feel the shift from rebellious discomfort to a sort of resigned flowing.

It seems to me that what may occur in these experiences that remains so distinct in memory is a resonant opening to transpersonal energy fields. There is a pattern of experience for me that recurs when I am trudging through snow and having a hard time of it. This pattern seems to tap into an extended experience of such difficulty—a field of resonance that may have something to do with past-life experience—or is simply an archetypal field of resonance. At those times I feel like a refugee, or a prisoner on a forced march, or someone like Dr. Zhivago struggling across the frozen tundra. There is a quality of desperate resignation that sometimes becomes transcendent.

These distinct, curiously loaded memories of what would seem mundane moments can be used as access points for transformative work. The memory or the recurring pattern can be approached within an altered state, and its component energies explored. This may yield insights relevant to present experience and teachings about alignment and work with resonant fields. Positive contributions to the energies of these transpersonal fields can have far-reaching effects.

Dreaming is also a state offering itself to transcendent work. If you ignore this precinct of consciousness as a practitioner, you put yourself at a disadvantage. "Night practice" is not only a mirror of daily patterns but is a realm of application unto itself. There is a great deal of literature available about dreaming. In these brief pages I will touch on a few considerations for the practitioner.

In looking at the patterns of your dreaming you will probably notice that there are periods in which you do not have much dream recall. You will likely also notice collections of dreams that follow a particular theme for a while then change to a new series, dreams that precede recurring dreams, and so on. The more you look at large patterns and correlate them to what is moving both above and below the surface of waking life, the more you can usefully work with and integrate various realms and states of consciousness.

Being observant of patterns gives you a sense of direction and context. Individual dreams, like individual days, are aspects of larger cycles. Having some understanding of the cycles—or at least an awareness of them—allows you to more effectively direct your spirit work.

Another thing to be aware of is the dreaming of those around you, or those you have close connections with. You may be intercepting other people's dreams. This sometimes happens not just with those you are close to, but with people for whom you are doing spiritual work. It may happen unintentionally; it may also occur as a deliberate link between you. Occasionally your dreams can contain messages for others who may be blocking their own dream reception.

Inadvertent impact on one another's dreams is not always useful. When I would compare dream notes with my son in the mornings, it was often obvious that one of us had affected the other's dreams either through unspoken preoccupations the day before, or through the dreams themselves. This is part of being mutually telepathic.

Sometimes the result of expanded consciousness is dreaming affected by movements of energy in the larger world. War or an earthquake or major political unrest or mass emotions of some kind can manifest through a sensitive person's dreams. With experience you can recognize these dreams for what they carry, and respond through compassionate work within expanded consciousness.

If you are psychically receptive, intrusive dreams may be visited upon you. No matter how blameless, innocuous, or careful you are in your work, if you are involving yourself with power or entering the realms beyond the ordinary, you will stir whatever feels threatened by your work. All strands are connected—when you touch one thread the entire web quivers.

When you ask for the attention of the spirits you also attract notice of the shadows. Doing healing work or shamanic journeying or even just prayer for someone involves you in their energies and whatever is attached to their personal matrices. As long as you tend to your clearing practices and maintain a strong alignment to Spirit, there should be no problem. But shadows finding resonance with something unattended inside of you will be able to manifest their influences on many levels, including your dreams. If you find this happening, it makes sense to do healing work for yourself, to give more attention to clearing and alignment, and to protect yourself as necessary during this process. This may lead to changes in how you operate in your practice as well.

Friends and family can be touched by these side effects of your work, so dreaming is no small matter. Dreams are often a vulnerable opening into your inner realms, but can also be the level at which you are able to realize that something in your life is amiss. You can take heed of this to respond firmly and transformatively.

I once received bodywork from a man with the psychically "cleanest" hands I have ever seen. I asked him what he did to maintain himself this way. He described an intensive forty-five minute process, congruent with his path, that he undertook every time he finished giving someone a massage. The process involved chanting, chakra work, connecting with his guardian angels, and prayer. He employed this ritual in addition to his daily practices.

This kind of committed attention to clarity and alignment enables altered states to be used in healthy and powerful ways. It recognizes that in fluid states of awareness you need to carry an orientation that draws good to you and expresses good through you. The capacity to enter these states is not in itself a guarantee of benevolent interaction within them. It is not in itself a qualification for anything but further learning.

three

GUIDANCE

Intuition—attention to inner guidance and knowing—is a quality of the West. Strength and application of intuition are common to all practitioners of natural spirituality, since intuition is a native gift of consciousness. Its function is enhanced when the interpretive process within intuition is recognized and disarmed. This again involves the realization of how perception and projection intermingle. Perception, though influenced by habit, is engaged in immediate experience. Interpretation of what is perceived, however, uses beliefs and conjectures based on beliefs as its reference.

Intuition is one source of guidance. Relationship with sacred advisors is another, as is consultation with teachers or wise people on the physical plane. A third source of guidance is through divination focuses such as the tarot, I Ching, or rune stones. These intermediaries can help you align with intuition. They each have a particular language, and you may find an affinity to one or more of these languages, such as the imagery in a tarot deck or the intelligence of the I Ching. Divination marshals your concentration and orients your awareness to a perspective offering applicable insights. As always, interpretation will shape those insights in personal ways.

Like all good consultants, divination allies are there to aid you in locating your own compass, not to take over the job of pointing your way. Their use only opens perspective if your intuitional capacity is already functional; their presentations will otherwise be opaque.

This is true of any system of guidance. When the consultant—whether that be a divination ally, totem, religious text, human teacher, or whatever—becomes a repository for your unending need to be told how to proceed in life, the nature of your relationship limits your growth. For one thing, you are forgetting that what you truly need and are capable of is direct communication with Source. As well, it creates inappropriate dependencies, inhibiting your experience of the real potentials of relationship to guides.

Each consultant has certain strengths to share that help you grow into your abilities. Each guide has its known territory. In good relationship you honor the gifts, and realize their parameters are meant to encourage your continued movement into alignment with the source of knowing. Some years ago all my totems, though quite present, stopped talking to me until I recognized that I had become shortsighted in my guidance-seeking, foregoing my primary reference to the Mystery.

A phenomena of guidance that enjoys popularity in the New Age community is channeling. I attended a channeling session once, at the invitation of friends who wanted to know what this activity looked like from my point of view. The woman conducting this session channeled several disembodied beings from outside our galaxy, one after the other. Then she answered personal questions from the audience. During the channeling her voice and gestures were different for each of the beings "coming through."

What I saw was that her aura changed when she initially entered her channeling state. I did not sense any additional presences. It was not like shamanic spirit possession or traditional pagan or Native spirit impersonation, which have definite manifestations of presence.

As channeling has gotten more sophisticated it has been catagorized as either conscious or unconscious channeling; from there come other gradations of practice. My contact has been minimal, but a few characteristic aspects of channeling give me food for thought.

One feature of channeling is that it seems to place a high premium on disembodied-ness itself. As long as the being who is channeled is considered an "ascended master," or better yet, a spirit that never abided on this Earth, it is given a place of authority about how life here should be experienced. A subfeature of this is that what is channeled is never an animal, bug, or tree lichen. (Dolphin channeling seems to be the exception, due in great part to the belief that dolphins are really space beings.) This reflects a collective view that disembodied, "higher" forms are the guides most worthy of our attention. A Native elder once remarked, "Dead don't make you smart." Disembodied, whether because of death or chosen condition, is not necessarily a gauge of wisdom.

Another feature of New Age style channeling is its functional aim of guidance for the many, not just for the individual accessing what is channeled. Whether what is channeled is believed to be the channeler's "higher self," or Jesus Christ, or the Grand Wazir of the Pleiades, the directive is to instruct the receptive masses. The language in which channeling is expressed has an eerie sameness to it, regardless of the channeler and the being who is channeled. It sounds unctuous, stilted, cliché, patronizing, and indeed disembodied.

Channeling does not seem to include doing anything, such as healing. It seems strictly a matter of talk—presenting beliefs as truths from enlightened, but absent, authorities. Certainly new or rediscovered knowledge can come through. But there is a great deal of illusion, camouflaged ill beliefs, and confused alignments not being examined.

Who are the channelers? Are they Natives, Africans, Asians, Hispanics, elders, or poor people? The faces in the magazines and books tell me that the channelers are Caucasian, fashionably groomed baby boomers. What need is channeling fulfilling? What current through society is it mirroring?

Wherever you turn for guidance will be worthwhile if it is within a good relationship, and if you understand your guide's alignment. You can glean what is useful without binding yourself to an unconsidered trust or faith, whoever the consultant.

Sometimes it is beneficial to let there be periods when you are not guided. "Help me, show me, tell me, lead me," we often beseech in prayer. "Guide me." Guidance is always present. When you feel at a loss for direction, it may be a signal to sit down and take stock of where you are and what you are doing spiritually. Stillness may be more valuable at that time than knowing direction. If you are not being where you are it will not do you much good to move along—you will just continue being not where you are in some other place. Stillness reveals truths you need in present context, and your acceptance of those leads you to the guidance you seek for moving onward.

In practicing natural spirituality, where do you look for guidance? Mostly through the teachings of daily experience and the signposts of your core alignments. Suggestions can come from any consultant—totem, divination ally, natural omen, spirit guide, teacher, text, or human associate—but suggestions must always be utilized or set aside in reference to your core alignments. Your heart is the compass for this process. It can enlist the aid of your body (gut instincts) and your mind (translations, encouragement, mapmaking). Intuition has a wonderful simplicity to its directives. "Drive further down this road," it will say, or "Telephone your sister," or "Begin the ceremony with the Eagle song." Instinctual guidance is a great boon—its presence enables the practitioner to move with the surety and natural grace of a hunting falcon or leaping deer.

It is tempting to just cultivate and act from this intuitive basis, and to not tamper with its simplicity. Indeed, intuition is a valuable guide, but after decades of operating intuitively I found it important to go another step, into understanding. The process of understanding explores beneath intuition's directives. It asks, "What am I responding to?" and, "How do I know?" Understanding asks to see the true faces of its informants and to stand amid the inner workings of consciousness.

Seeking understanding is ultimately not a demystification process if mystery is at the core—if there is not a grasping need for explanation. Seeking understanding shows a willingness to draw closer to Mystery, to be a wiser agent of it by making use of the mind's capacity to orient toward Source.

Understanding and intuition can be partners, one fine-tuning the other. Sometimes one challenges the other, and this is instructive too.

It becomes a system of checks and balances as well as of stronger, more complete participation. The magic of intuition is not removed by understanding. Understanding does not have to be an intellectual analysis or lack of spontaneity. It does not have to crowd out or rationalize intuition. It is just another aspect of knowing. It helps you to see things that lead to greater knowing and broadens your practice, moving you across wide spiritual terrains that otherwise might never be approached.

Sometimes when discussing guidance people will say, "My totem (or some other spirit) told me to do this." This sort of relationship with guidance may be problematic if it is based on projection or illusion or if it chronically—perhaps conveniently—lacks understanding. For sure there are times when you need to move purely on trust or faith—I do not question this time-honored response to spiritual guidance. But when spirits tell people to do things that have no resonance with personal or larger well-being, I have to wonder if it is truly guidance from Spirit. It is easy to displace accountability; it's like saying "The Devil made me do it." Unacknowledged needs or desires may play themselves out through projections of spirit guidance. It is also possible that a guide may actually suggest something in order for those fixated needs or desires to be externalized.

The process of understanding is not without illusion either. In trying to comprehend life's unfoldment people tend to make tidy packages out of encounters and experiences: "I had a baby on that certain night so I could meet the taxi driver who became my guru." Or "The tree fell on my ankle so I could learn to love myself with a prosthetic foot." The "so" conjunction is the tip-off that you are making a small, self-absorbed world out of complex, interdependent causes. This is typical of ego.

If you change the "so" to "and," you gain a truer perspective. The baby, the taxi driver, and the falling tree all have their own agendas of which you are only one aspect, and the forces at work, possible choices, and understandings to be derived are legion. Guidance and understanding are both richly multilayered.

Guides that can speak wisely in everyone's language are those manifesting life's beauty. Acquaintance with them comes through attending to what is around you. The tumbling creek talks of good cheer, refreshment for all, and participation in a sparkling network of life in motion. The brief, stunning colors of sunset speak of a fullness of expression regardless of your time on this Earth. The cat stretched in the sunshine reminds you to partake of exquisite, commonplace pleasures, to live with satisfaction and grace. The stark desert tells of patience, timing, and acceptance. The hardy plantain pushing through the sidewalk crack advises you to make each opportunity a habitat for growth.

When listening to these guides you find harmony in their messages; they do not argue with one another no matter their differences. You begin to know them as one guide—the voice of love speaking through life. It speaks through the snowflake, and through the earthquake, and through the mechanic working on your truck's carburetor. Relationship to guidance should be relationship to love—a teaching of heart as well as mind.

four

HEALING

Minutes before sitting down to write this chapter, I burned my hand while putting logs into the woodstove. My first response was a moderate expletive aimed at my clumsiness. Next was putting hand to mouth, cooling the burn with saliva, followed by walking to the kitchen to ask an aloe plant for a leaf tip to salve the burn.

Healing is restoration of implicit well-being. The mundane example of the burn shows one path this might take. The first response was a recognition (albeit a judgmental one) of what had occurred and why. I had not been well positioned to juggle the heavy logs, and was not giving full attention to the task. In this was a pattern of incomplete physical awareness and care. In the expletive was a pattern of annoyance at the body for not functioning with independent competency. Part of the healing process (though not always the initial response) is to see what has contributed to disruption of well-being. Ideally, this is done without blame.

The second response was to comfort myself. This can (and in this case did) include forgiveness of self and others, release of negative emotions, and intelligent first aid to the body. Release and comfort help you not lock in energies of harm.

Lastly, in this example, I went to the aloe plant (took steps to actively assert a healing intention); asked in a respectful, grateful way for its medicine to assist me (opened to connectedness with healing and with allies); and applied the herb's juices to the burn (accepted its image of my wholeness).

Physically, healing may take time to become apparent or there may be more that needs to be addressed through the focus of disturbance, but in basic terms the healing in this situation had been carried out. In this example I might ponder the significance of the interaction—what imbalances were being expressed through the painful encounter with the fire, or the woodstove, or the work of heating the house. I might consider if there is anything meaningful about what part of me got burned in the incident. I might become motivated to be more attentive around this kind of physical task, or to cultivate more strength and balance, or to find a different way of heating the house. All this could be part of the healing.

This process sounds more laborious than it is. Because I note patterns and try to make everyday use of this awareness, it was natural to immediately recognize some of the forces at work in this incident. Because I would rather deal with patterns in their small manifestations than in major disruptions of well-being, I try to apply a healing awareness to even minor events. And because good, transformative alliances are something valued in life, I am conscious of nurturing relationship with allies.

This is all part of natural spirituality—the integration of body and spirit in daily living. When your spirituality is not dogmatic, you need to learn from what is present and apply your practice to opportunities at hand.

Healing usually involves a dual process of removing harmful influences and restoring connection to well-being. This is similar to the clearing process for objects that I described in an earlier chapter. Success is often determined by your capacity to see wholeness regardless of influences obscuring it. As with objects, it is usually easier to do this with others than with yourself. Healing has a lot more to do with love than with achieving conventional states of health.

The process of identifying and clearing harmful influences may be addressed on many levels: physical influences, mental formations, negative emotions, psychic energies, or combinations of these. As a practitioner you may have a particular starting place or access, or particular levels you are more aware of than others. You may approach the healing process through symptoms or spirit guides—it makes no difference as long as all levels are eventually included.

Depending on the situation, some of the levels will not be as influential as others. The work of clearing requires varying degrees of understanding these influences and how they are causing harm.

The second phase of healing is restoration of well-being. If you have the skills (and permission), you can restructure energies at a core level, calling upon an implicit intelligence of function to manifest. This is more radical than just moving energies around. It rearranges things at the premanifestation level. Here you are in communication with the causal body.

In any healing work it is important to include release, alignment with well-being, and gratitude. How these are enacted is an individual matter.

Healing allies are often part of practice. A drug prescription can be approached the same way as other allies. In taking a pill you can address the essence of that form. You can speak to it respectfully as a medicine helper, and describe your desires and intentions to it. You are bringing it into your intimate space, hoping for its powers to benefit you. Why not treat it in a way that is congruent with your spirituality? Smudge your pills. Put them on your altar. If you are ambiguous about using them, come to terms with this relationship in a sacred way.

Treat all your healing allies in a sacred manner, whether they are herbs, stones, prescription drugs, foods, or acupuncture needles. Herbs—plant medicines—have re-emerged as healers in modern society. Using them in the same way allopathic practitioners use drugs (this treats this; this cures that) is missing the plant family's deeper teachings and applications to healing. Even if your philosophy is more holistic than allopathic, you still may be thinking in terms of illness, not wellness.

Each herb has its unique perspective of wellness that is part of the Earth's wellness. If you have a sense of how that uniqueness affirms your (or someone else's) wellness, you can invoke the medicine of that plant's expression of wholeness. The aloe, for example, offers me a vision of self that is cool, that has integrity of surfaces, that is nourished through transformation. When I invoke its medicine I see myself through those eyes, through that perspective of wellness. I call for its unique mirror to restore my vision of wholeness.

To know what that uniqueness may include, you inquire into what aspect of the Earth's wellness the plant embodies. This not only gives clues about how that medicine can be applied to healing, it also reminds you that plants have their own purposes and lives beyond human use. Healing is only one of their engagements with being.

Another path of learning about herbs is of course through the direct relationship of alliance—through communication. The properties or physical explanations of a plant's effects hardly begin to describe its nature and medicine. The longer you work with a plant— the more you attend to its teachings, and to the quality of its presence—the more you realize that, like all good allies, the strength of its being itself helps you to be yourself, in wellness.

The aloe mirrors wholeness in my consciousness; it also speaks directly to the cells of my body in a specific language, helping the body remember and manifest wholeness. The aloe's fragrance or taste or texture may speak to my emotions in a way needed to realign them with wholeness, so in the act of invoking the aid of this plant ally I can reconnect all aspects of my being with wellness.

If herbal healing is your focus, you may become increasingly sensitive to the uniqueness of each plant, and to each plant's resonance with certain people or situations. If healing itself is your focus, you may gradually move into a relationship where plants lend themselves to your intentions regardless of their properties. In this alliance you call upon their core life forces rather than the particularity of their medicine—their Selfness rather than their selfness. I believe that, in order to do this respectfully, you must first know and honor their selfness. It is like the work with your own awareness of being: to not be arrogant or disconnected in your expanded consciousness of Self, you need to tend to the embodied teachings of self.

One level of alliance with the plants nourishes and informs the other. It seems especially important in today's world for people to connect with plants, animals, stones, and so on as individual beings worth getting humbly acquainted with. Taking time to know a mullein from a burdock, to be able to greet it by name when you see it, and to have knowledge of its medicine is a step toward realizing harmonious participation within the community of life. This, too, is an aspect of healing. By moving out of the "user" role into natural, healthy interdependencies, you further the restoration of well-being.

Love is where healing truly takes place, because without it there cannot be wellness. Love can transcend or transform all other conditions. There is often an image of wellness that is tied to certain expressions of health or to certain outcomes of destiny. These images can hinder healing by putting restrictions on what is accepted.

Illness, injury, pain, and death are not enemies. Not even fear is an enemy. Accepting wellness is accepting that which is called into service of wellness on your path of healing. As you move with this, your path may change. But wellness is not a goal—an ultimate condition. It is an alignment accepting love, accepting truth, accepting being. Each moment of doing this is a moment of wellness, a homecoming.

five

TOUCH

There are moments in the writing of these chapters when I wish it could all be done without words. So much of what healing is about is better conveyed by touch. A friend asked me to do some healing work for him. He lay on the floor and I sat beside him, becoming still inside, waiting for the right action to arise and guide me. When it did I reached out and gently grasped my friend's feet; he took a deep breath and started to cry.

All the love in the world can be expressed in a touch. People go to healers mostly to be touched in a nurturing, transformative way. That is one of the grievous aspects of modern health systems—they are so machine- and drug-oriented, so technological, harsh, and cold. Nurses sometimes try to make up for the impersonal handling of doctors (who often feel required to be impersonal), but the aberrances that have marred our trust in touch make contact with one another risky.

My father, who was surrounded through most of life with the uptight attitudes about touch typical of his class and generation, now basks in the warmth of such therapies as massage, craniosacral adjustment, and therapeutic touch. One of the things he likes best about these is that the practitioners always hug him good-bye at the session's end.

I am not a promiscuous hugger (except of baby animals), but when such contact can be enacted with mindfulness and clear heart, it nurtures connection to love. Many of us are responsive to the amount of good touching children need, and yet we forget how much grownups need it too. Human touch is not the only resource for nourishing contact. There may be times when it is the caress of sun and breeze that heals—the touch of cool springy moss, or the stroking waters of a lake that soothes your isolation. It may be the rough-and-tumble play with a shaggy dog, or the warm velvety cat asleep in your arms that are the contacts making you feel at ease and connected to life. Or it may be you need to touch yourself, with kindness and delight.

Healing touch is of the West because it shares, connects to love, and sometimes takes away what hurts; the parent's hands comfort, guide, join, protect. In the East are the child's hands, taking things apart, investigating them. In the South the lover's hands arouse, endear, expose. In the North the hands of wisdom build, give, and transmit, carrying remembrance of all times.

If you use your hands for healing, you need to take care of them as medicine conduits. This entails keeping them cleared, sensitive, and open to flows of healing energy. Massage your hands. Smudge and ceremoniously cleanse them. Work with opening the hand chakras on your palms, and use a stone or your fingernails to break up crystallization in your fingertips. Practice breathing and meditation techniques that circulate or concentrate energy in your hands. Aikido wrist exercises help open the hand channels and build strength and flexibility.

I remember how strong my hands were when I was a homesteader and midwife. Milking a flock of goats twice a day was perfect exercise for the hands. Midwifery is mostly touch work. In midwifery your hands become like another pair of eyes, going where your visual perception cannot. I knew a midwife who arrived at the birth of a baby whose parents were both blind. It was night, and the house was without lights. There was no time to go buy a flashlight or candles, so the midwife assisted the delivery in the dark, purely by touch.

When you align with the power of love and focus awareness in your hands, healing intention can be conveyed and amplified through touch. There is a close relationship between emotional feelings and physical feelings. If you are out of touch with your emotions, try keying into your body (or vice versa). In the midst of any given situation, you might have a sense of disconnection from what you are feeling, but you can get direct messages from your body. You can check in with your bodily sensations—tension, adrenaline flow, exhaustion, stiffness, sexual arousal, comfort, and so on—and track them inward to emotional levels of feeling and response.

Experiment with different postures and with how you feel when assuming them, or focus on a series of different states such as confidence, wariness, receptivity, and so on, spontaneously moving into postures that express each of those states. These exercises can help you align sensation with emotion, and their teachings applied to situations where you want to be clearer in your participation.

Touch is a primary aspect of sexuality, which is why spiritual celibates do not do much touching. Intimate touch is an area of widespread abuse. How does a practitioner reconcile sexual nature with work? Is repression the answer? Or perhaps making sexuality more explicit? Abuse of touch raises questions about our ways of relating to each other and to the primal forces moving within sexuality. Instead of approaches that either repress sexuality or project it into hands-on healing practices, perhaps we can walk a more middle path.

What makes the massage you give your lover different from the one you give your client? It is what you do with your hands—where and how your touch moves—that is guided by the different natures of the two relationships. The other thing that makes the massages different is the active presence or absence of sexual intention or charge. Good relationship abides within mutual respect, agreements, and trust.

What if your client is someone to whom you have a sexual response? Now what? Is it time to repress? Confess? Pretend you are not taking sexual pleasure from the contact? Repression tends to deaden touch, making it mechanical, disconnecting it from vital energies. Deliberately hiding your pleasure can range from a fairly harmless secret to a deep violation of trust and safety boundaries. It can amount to a sleazy rip-off. Confession may relieve guilty feelings, but then what?

A more honest and whole way to work with such situations is to recognize that sexual energies are part of embodiment. They are natural and sacred. Your sexuality is a medicine bundle—there are times for it to be open and times for it to be wrapped. When it is wrapped it is still there, on your inner altar, but its energies are not invoked into movement and influence. Your recognition and honoring of sexuality is different from repression, which is fearful and divides you from yourself. You can remain aware of and connected to your sexuality without inappropriately expressing its power in another's personal space.

As a midwife and in my healing work, I have had contact with people's most intimate physical parts. In midwifery I saw that, though heterosexual, I have a deep appreciation for women's bodies. Through healing work I learned that I can admire, touch, love, and even experience attraction without catalyzing sexual energies that impose on those occasions. My sexuality may or may not awaken through touching someone, but if it awakens it can stay motionless and within. In this state of peace it usually just goes back to sleep. It leaves me free to see the naked, laboring woman with her wonderful hills and curves as beautiful; to see the man undressing for the sweat, his back muscles graceful in the firelight, as beautiful and go no further than that. The medicine bundle stays wrapped. There is no violation.

If your relationship with sexuality becomes clear of neediness and shadows, this medicine bundle can be worked with more actively. Along with containing the elements of your personal sexuality, this bundle is charged with primal energies of life. These forces, when undistorted by abusive patterns and ill beliefs, are healing, enlivening, and creative. They are vital energies in medicine work.

The awareness that needs to be cultivated in this work is an awareness of how ego can get confused about these energies—of how ego can get power hungry—and can use generative forces in degenerative ways. Because of the struggles men and women are working through within duality's context, these energies of union and transformation can greatly challenge clarity of relationship. Most patterns of belief and behavior are not yet aligned with a perspective enabling primal energies to be used without shadow or confusion.

As the way we touch is healed, the way we touch will carry healing. One lack I felt in my childhood stemmed from my mother's Christian Science orientation. The religion of Christian Science focuses on correcting erroneous thought rather than addressing the physical appearance of illness. While my mother was intelligently engaged with the causative realm, I yearned to be touched when I felt bad—to be held, comforted, ministered to, brought out of pain's isolation. The body is a place of manifestation, an aspect of Earthly experience, a place love can be received and expressed.

Touch should never be underestimated or used carelessly. In natural spirituality, it is another of your native, powerful gifts, one whose use asks most clearly for integrity within love.

CRISIS AND LIMBO

Crisis—too much happening at once!—or limbo—nothing happening for too long!—are states you may experience from time to time. They are meant to be transitional states, not ongoing life conditions. They are also not states to dread.

Some of you fire signs might find crisis stimulating rather than daunting, but even those who thrive on the intensities of crisis will admit that the stresses involved can throw you off center. What purpose does crisis serve? Imagine life, as it currently manifests, without crisis, and what would happen if we never had crisis. A lot of repressed and unaddressed, unending, undermining, unresolved problems is what we would have. Crisis brings things to the surface. It confronts, demanding active response. It erupts through procrastination and pretense. It gets in your face. I am not fond of crisis, but I have to admit it is an effective disrupter of the stagnant status quo. It is the party crasher, the coyote in the henhouse, the rattler in the woodpile, the one thing you did not want to happen.

Looking back to the description of how beliefs move into the West's fluid realm and are disarranged, you can see a parallel with external crisis. Stable structures of belief are dissolved, energy freed and then restructured or otherwise used. In crisis the stability of a situation dissolves, energies run free and are then dissipated or reconfigured. If stability is tenuous, further crisis will probably not be long in manifesting.

Like the destructuring of belief, the external crisis provides opportunity for alignments to change. As with emotional charges holding beliefs together, so the emotional charges holding situations together will release through crisis. This release may be the most stressful aspect of crisis, as intense emotions may indeed ensue, but if you instead manage to cram emotions back into place, you suffer the high price of their forced containment. People not worried about emotional restraint will vent uninhibitedly in such situations, but is this healthy either?

There are many opinions about how to deal with emotions. Indiscriminate venting seems to me abusive in its emotional violence and in its tendency to be loaded with accumulated energies that are not specific to the situation at hand. Venting also tends to dig deeper the ruts through which anger courses. Suppression and control are not productive alternatives. Transformation—changing feelings as you change patterns—may be the best option. Moderate doses of venting and control may support this process if done within a context of awareness.

Instead of shrieking, "You stupid bitch!" you might shout, "I'm angry, leave me alone for awhile!" Then go walk off some of the energy, and instead of using your mind to feed the anger, use it to calm down and realign to love's options. Crisis can reveal and dislodge energies. You can use it to expose instead of intensify misunderstandings. What good is all that distress if it only becomes the eruptive part of a repetitious cycle of suffering? Allow crisis to be a transformative context. Make positive choices. Take action. Realign scattered energies to form foundations for healthy relationships. Take advantage of crisis to get an honest look at what has been buried or hidden. Put your spiritual commitment into practice.

Just writing about crisis makes the thought of limbo rather appealing, but this state can be as difficult for some people as crisis is for others. Times of limbo are those when you feel at a loss for direction, momentum, or life focus. It is a sense of suspension. Context lacks cohesion or continuity. Inspiration and energy are low, or have no apparent path of manifestation. You might feel alternately restless and dulled. Inner voices nag at you or are frustratingly silent; your life may seem uselessly cluttered or despairingly empty. Limbo is the great between. You wait, or fret, or try to fill it, or break out of it. Nothing seems to flow.

Limbo, like crisis, is an opportunity for change, though it expresses itself differently. Both interrupt your habitual procedure through life. With limbo you have the luxury of a less intense context in which to ponder and put changes in motion, but without the pressure of crisis it may be hard to motivate your participation.

In the chapter on guidance this directionless time was mentioned as a valuable period for looking at where you are, for becoming present and realizing what is there. It lets your spirit, mind, and body catch up with one another and take counsel together. It allows integration and acceptance.

The experience of not going anywhere, not making plans to go anywhere, and not knowing when you will or where it will be or how you will get there is terrifying (or depressing) if you need a sense of proceeding toward a goal in order to feel secure. If you are used to seeing ahead, or even just to moving intuitively without interruption, the suspension in limbo will be disconcerting.

When people come to me describing this state and how they feel as though they have lost their clarity, I tell them how great this is. Clarity is tricky in that it can lead to complacency—like getting a weather forecast on Monday and relying on its being applicable for the entire week. Clarity is tricky in other ways too. Things like the need to be certain can disguise themselves as clarity. Limbo brings all this to a halt. Even real clarity may need to shift focus for a time if you are neglecting to apply it to all areas of your life. Or you may need to develop some other capacity besides clarity—like trust, or patience, or a more interdependent attitude.

Limbo can be a time of integration, a time of being present and a time of cultivating new strengths. Most people are less likely to make changes when they are in motion than when they feel stalled. Motion gives an impression that all systems are go, and that everything is functional if not entirely satisfactory. In limbo there may be a greater willingness to consider change, and to see things in a different light. A memorable limbo time for me was when I got a divorce, put my belongings in storage, sent my son and our companion animals to visit family, and set off to find a new home. There came a point when prospects were dim and I had no clue how to proceed. I was out of money; I had no job, no home, failing health, and I was alone.

One evening I stopped at a highway rest area to spend the night in my car. As I wrapped a blanket around myself and lay back, watching the stars appear, I considered my situation. It seemed bleak, but I didn't feel bleak. Something came to rest within my heart, like a bird weary from the flying but still alive. Alive beneath the stars, and belonging to an interconnected universe of life. It came to rest, and as it did something else lifted and flew free. I had, at that moment, such a sense of peace. The limbo did not scare me; in fact, it felt just fine. In it were nested all kinds of unknown possibilities.

When you are on a narrow track you tend to put on blinders that may help you focus on the path before you but block your view of other direction. However, when you let go of fears and fixations, you realize that the suspension of limbo has increased your awareness of possibilities. Your impetus is slowed down enough that you can choose to change course or to continue on your path with new perspective.

Times of crisis and limbo come naturally in everyone's lives, like frothing rapids and quiet eddies in a river. The skilled paddler does not portage around them. The wise journeyer does not cover the eyes during rapids, or disdain opportunities for rest and a look at the scenery in the quiet backwaters.

The rhythm of life shifts in the way seasons shift. Life's pace is not a mechanical sameness. Some seasons may be more congenial to you than others, but to fear the shifting rhythms is to forget the gifts of each and the way life is strengthened by each. If winter or summer went on forever, it would destroy well-being. The same would happen if crisis or limbo become perpetual in your life. They are exaggerations of life's rhythm, and their occurrences are times to transform patterns and move in new ways.

seven

DEATH

It is late November and winter has come to the mountain. The day has a nightlike silence and stillness. I lean against the wall of the house and watch snow gently but inexorably cover the land, cover the garden, cover what is familiar and beloved. I know all will return in another season, though changed, but watching in the quiet afternoon as winter shrouds what is known to me I feel a passing, and say good-bye.

In the days of my midwifery practice I had an apprentice-assistant named Allysia. She had a troubled life, and eventually left her husband and two sons and went to the city. Her friends missed her and worried about her, but never heard from her until word came that she had been raped and stabbed to death one night in a Chicago park. I was asked to conduct a ceremony to help her friends say good-bye and somehow cope with the brutality of this death.

In the ceremony we spoke of our love for this woman and shared memories emblematic of each person's relationship with her, or their particular sense of who she was. We sang and sent prayers for Allysia's journey in the spirit world. We addressed feelings about the man who killed her, about the society that gave context for that act, and about our own fears and vulnerabilities.

Tears flowed throughout the ceremony. At the end a woman suddenly, startlingly, spoke up. Of all the people present, she was the most emotionally controlled. She always seemed calm, contained, correct in her behavior. I never heard her shout. But now she spoke sharply, nakedly. "I feel unfinished in this. I am angry at Allysia. I am angry! She wouldn't let us help her; she held it all inside, then went where this horrible thing happened to her, where no one could help her, leaving us with this anguish!"

I once did a three-hour sweat lodge, and when it ended everyone went out but one. That person said she felt a need to sweat longer; would it be permitted? I closed the door flap and we continued for another three hours. In the same way, this ceremony for our friend's passing continued until it was truly done.

The anguish death can bring is not something simply dispensed with by ceremony or anything else, but feelings—even selfish, "unacceptable" feelings—that bind anguish to the heart can be expressed and released.

Sometimes help is asked for and given, bringing anguish of a different kind. This past autumn my sweetheart and I sat reading in the failing light of afternoon, enjoying the quiet of the mountain, the dog and cats relaxing near us. Suddenly—bang!—a furry body flung itself against the picture window. I rushed to the window to look. An intense, golden-eyed face stared up at me: a bobcat. She withdrew, and I darted to another vantage. The wildcat peered at me again, this time from around the edge of some straw bales. Her face riveted my gaze—those lighted eyes; the ears with their high, tufted tips.

She drew back and I went outside, catching sight of her at the base of the garden. She turned once more to look at me, pulling at my heart, and vanished over the lip of the hillside.

I did not follow. Because she was a being of the wilds, I did not think she would want me to. The reason for her behavior remained a puzzle.

Night passed, and another day. Night came again; it was cold, the ground patchy with snow. I rose in the morning and there she was, lying on her side in the garden, dead. I went to her, stunned. She had not been dead long. How beautiful her fur—soft and thick, shaded and marked with russet, gray, black, cream. To my horror I saw what excitement had blinded me to the day she had first come. Both paws on the right side were gone, chewed off, the front one at the first leg joint, the other higher up. Both stumps were scabbed over—this had happened many days before her death.

When I lifted her body it was almost weightless. She had died of starvation. Brave little wild one, she had come to me for help despite the reclusive nature of bobcats, despite the presence of the dog, but I had not recognized her need. It broke my heart—I would have been so glad to help her.

I smudged her body and made prayers. We buried her in the garden where her Earthly time had ended, putting tobacco with her, and a little milk for her spirit journey. I could not find the leghold trap that had so cruelly gripped her, though I did come upon the bootprints of the trapper. For a time I found it hard to forgive either of us.

"She knew where to go," a friend said later, when I spoke of the bobcat's ordeal.

"But it did her no good," was my thought in reply. "I failed her." This is a grief that is sometimes part of death, too; the feeling that love is not enough if it fails to prevent or forestall death. The pain of this can be unending, but if you do not let it go I think you may bind the journeying spirit, as well as yourself, to the very suffering you long to have prevented. As the snow deepened over this brave cat's grave I gave my grief to winter's healing.

My sweetheart was also with me when I came upon a swallow lying in the road after a car had smacked into it. We stopped, and when I went to the bird I heard in my mind a distinct command: "Get me off this road, now!" It was startling—I thought the bird was already dead.

We sat on the riverbank beside the road. A Reiki practitioner, my sweetheart asked if I would like him to hold the bird. A close look gave me no doubt that the bird was dying. He asked if I wanted him to end the bird's suffering, to speed its passage. I hesitated, wanting to know what was right to do. "Wait a little," I said.

As we watched, it immediately became clear that this bird wanted to die in its own way. It struggled upright in my sweetheart's cupped hands, spread its wings, arched its back, and with an intense end-to-end quiver seemed to unloose its spirit and send it flying out its opened beak.

In the moment of this act I sensed a large, birdlike spirit form hovering over the river, felt the shadow of it over us. The swallow's brightness of being seemed to soar up and be taken into this form, like child to parent, then both were gone. The tiny body seemed empty, and the air around us held nothing but sunlight.

With animal companions or with wild creatures, there are times when you are faced with choosing to speed death or to let it come at its own pace. Suffering may indeed degrade quality of life, and you may be called upon to bring death in order for suffering to end. But it is an individual matter—what each creature needs is different.

If you project your need for pain to end, either because you cannot stand to witness suffering, or because you would not want your life prolonged if you were in suffering, you may take lives that are not finished. Likewise, if you cannot bring yourself to respond to a request for a speedy death, either personally or by getting assistance, you may not truly be serving love. Either way, it is not an easy thing to know to do. It may indeed be the most difficult aspect of good relationship.

My friend François asked me to be his medicine person and "midwife" in the years during which he was dying of cancer, and many were the teachings of that experience. One to be shared here is the gift of community his dying brought forth.

François lived in a yurt during the last months of his illness. Friends rotated bringing him meals and spending nights with him. Toward the end a friend who was also a hospice worker moved in with him full-time. People brought him books, read to him, came up with exotic food treats they hoped would tempt his appetite, gave him beautiful crystals, and presented him with the newest (or oldest) natural treatments for cancer they could unearth. (He had already unsuccessfully undergone surgery, radiation, and chemotherapy.) François was only twenty-nine. Everyone wanted him to live.

François once told me, "People come and say how good I'm looking, or how bad I am looking, and it never has anything to do with how I really feel." François was seen by people as an incredibly gentle, artistic, spiritual person; now, in his otherworldly pallor and thinness, his dark eyes large and lucent, he was seen almost as an icon or saint. Visits were exhausting for him. Many people had an unacknowledged need for François to bestow some link for them with the beyond, and yet not really leave.

Despite this, what was paramount was the wholeheartedness of care administered to François—natural and spontaneous, given with good cheer. It brought people together through love. People became more genuine in their relationships, and much kinder. They made more direct eye contact, more conscious touch, and peace with those with whom they had differences.

François passed from this world surrounded by love. His children and their mother were beside him, and so were his friends. He passed gently, amid community. We prepared his body in a sacred way for its burning, and many people came to the yurt that night to pay respects, meditate a while, and say good-bye. His wife and friends transported the body to the crematorium and brought back the ashes. We scattered them on the breast of the ocean, boats full of friends singing as the ashes sank through the swells. Bright flower petals floated alongside the thousand tiny paper cranes the community had folded during his illness.

The next night was François's birthday. There was a gathering with music and feasting, a joyful remembrance. More than a hundred people were there, grateful for one another's company, and in the love so fully present, François was present also.

I have had my own times of acknowledging death's nearness, each time different. Once there was a vortex where pain and fear vanished and only a great acceptance remained. I remember another time, a presence in the darkness ready to take me across, and my heart crying out: "No, I am not finished, I realize my commitment." I remember one time drifting from the body—so still it was, and wasted, so small its flame—and wandering on the incense smoke of the funeral ghats in Benares.

In the West of the wheel, death is a breathing out, an unclenching hand. It is transformation's threshold. The passage speaks much about Earthly teachings, and much about the Mystery.

Osprey nest
full of snow,
the trees around it
bowing under white.
Again the cycle
gives us North—
will we bend
or break this time?
The beauty,
ache and clench
of tired body, both familiar and
impenetrable—
small fire within
with which to meet
this power.
The mountains become
stronger in winter,
the snow their shaman's
cloaks, clouds and gale
their spirit allies.
This land
speaks to me, asks
what medicine
I have brought
this time.

PART FOUR

North
Stone

one

EARTH

The presence of Earth in the North of the medicine wheel is not just seen in its aspects of practicality, groundedness, and manifestation. If you have ever been to the northern wilderness in winter you know another aspect, one of ethereal, crystalline beauty—magical, beyond grasping. The essence of the North's earthiness is the massive buffalo; it is also the silk-feathered owl. It is granite and it is diamond; it is the frozen lake of the past and the subtle smoke of sweetgrass blessing the newborn.

Earth is a Direction unto itself—the sacred home we stand upon. In this part of the North discussion, I would like to talk about good relationship with the Earth. (I am choosing not to discuss bad relationship with the Earth here.)

This discussion could be divided into four primary perspectives. The first is that of appreciation. Those who appreciate the Earth observe and admire the Earth's forms and varieties of expression. They experience being near the Earth.

The second perspective is that of stewardship. Stewards see the Earth as under their care and needful of them. They want to heal the Earth, wisely manage and use its resources, and behave benevolently to its denizens. They experience being on the Earth.

The third perspective is partnership. Partners see the Earth as a web of interrelationship in which they participate. They regard the human role as no greater or lesser than any other, and see all beings as belonging to the web, in harmonious cohabitation. They experience being with the Earth.

The last perspective is that of union. Those united with the Earth see it as Self. Their awareness is of both the particle and the wave in which Earth participates. They experience being Earth.

These four perspectives can be summed up in this way: Appreciation is an opening of awareness. Stewardship is an awakening of responsibility (albeit egocentric). Partnership is a recognition of kinship. Union is an enlargement of self. Some people stay within one of these perspectives all their lives. Some combine or fluctuate between several.

It may be useful to examine your own perspective. If you have an urge to save the world, consider what basis your urge is coming from. For example, an appreciator may look at the rain forest as a fascinating ecosystem, and judge it worth preserving. The steward may be concerned with what destruction of the forest will do to its treasure trove of medicinal herbs. The partner may decry the disrespect for life that is implicit in human destructiveness, and the person experiencing union with the rain forest may feel, within themselves, shifts of energy the Earth makes in response to this destruction.

Many people find inspiration visiting the Earth's recognized power centers. It is through local connection with habitat, however, that you learn to practice right relationship with the Earth. A basic premise of natural spirituality is that bringing sacredness into ordinary life is a path of healing for all.

What can be experienced in day-to-day encounters? Driving home one afternoon, I saw an eagle flying toward me from the mountainside. On the one hand, I saw the eagle going about its business—perceiving this through my senses and mental process. On the other hand, I even more vividly saw the eagle with my heart. When it glided off the mountainside, its head and tail feathers bright in the cold winter light, my heart opened like wings unfolding. There was no sense of separation from the eagle, or from the mountain, the sky, the light, and the small herd of buffalo standing in the snow beneath the eagle's glide.

Every time you open and see with the heart you are filled with medicine, with gratitude and love. My mother used to tell me, "You're always the one to see things." This is not because I am special. It is because life knows a heart that will open to it; life knows a heart's yearning. When a sense of kinship is there, the extended family keeps in touch, knows when you are lonely, speaks to you, comes to you.

A great deal of seeing or not seeing is predicated on habits of attention. Attention that is oriented toward birds, animals, trees, rocks, rainbows will see them. After talking about bird totems on the first day of a workshop, people often return the next day amazed at all the birds they saw on the drive home. Your particular inner focus draws outward response and orients your attention.

It is through connecting with local habitat that you begin learning how to be part of that environment in a harmonious way. You learn to participate, and to access the medicine available through harmony. You and your habitat start taking good care of each other in natural, integrated ways. This may deepen to a unified expression—a oneness of being. In complete integration, caring for yourself is caring for the habitat, and vice versa. There is no division of well-being or needs. You operate, then, from a unified consciousness of sacred intelligence. Right action becomes a natural instinct. The more you know the land, the more you see with the heart.

This way of seeing expands communication. You listen as you would to your own thoughts. If there is clarity in the heart—a depth of attunement—this will not involve projection. When I encounter an eagle, for instance, it may communicate its individual eagle-ness by flying off at my arrival, or express to me its feelings about the situation in some other way. The eagle's response can be either a personal communication that I hear in my thoughts or something more in the realm of species-to-species communication, a response between species sharing the same habitat that is based on a history of experience and relationship.

On this same occasion (or on another) the eagle could communicate Eagle-ness itself: The medicine—the particular truth—of Eagle may be conveyed in a generalized or personal way. On a third possible level of interaction, Spirit may speak through the eagle with a message, an understanding, or an experience. A fourth level is when encounter with the eagle opens awareness of the whole web, a powerful experience of interconnectedness.

Living in solitude with my companion animals I have also experienced a telepathic level of communication with them—a mutual sensitivity wherein thoughts and feelings are easily transmitted. This level of attunement can be unnerving sometimes.

If you live in the city, you are not shut out from connection to habitat. Beyond its usual denizens, more and more wild creatures are venturing into settled areas. As natural habitats are taken over by human development, there is little choice for wild creatures but to look for a living where they can find it. Connections need to be restored in every habitat, including cities.

In Seattle, a pair of peregrines made a nest on an upper-story ledge of a bank building. The bank put a closed-circuit camera in the window, and many people became absorbed in the drama of falcon life. Eggs were laid and hatched, pigeons were preyed upon and brought to the young falcons, and when the mama falcon died midseason, a surrogate was brought in by the state Wildlife Department to help father falcon care for the young. One baby died and one fledged.

It was a saga that captured many hearts. Daily, people gathered around television sets in the bank to watch the falcons. It was a strange sort of involvement, once removed (and best so), but feelings were engaged in a positive way, nourishing connectedness between humans and life's matrix.

All these levels of communication rely on your being open and attentive. If you are mainly used to species-to-species communication, you may need to make radical shifts in perspective in order for other levels to be accessed. If you are used to metaphorical relationships to other species, it may help to gain some field experience. The more time you spend with trees, stones, animals, and natural habitats, the clearer communication becomes. It takes patience. Human communication is oriented to such a narrow range of expression and reception that different or more subtle channels may take practice to develop. Part of this process is connecting with other humans on new levels as well. Perception can gradually become more sensitive and cast a wider net. You might find that you become a quieter—but not a less communicative—person.

two

Maintenance

As a spiritual practitioner, what are some ways to maintain yourself as you go about your work? Looking at the elements of the four Directions, you are presented with a balanced round of approaches for clearing and maintaining well-being.

In the East you have the medicine of Air, utilized in smudging and prayer. A prayer of gratitude for life each morning when you awake is one of the simplest ways you can honor well-being. It changes attitude for the better and draws blessing to the day's unfoldment. Prayer can be offered at meals and other times also, bringing return to center and present moment, nudging you out of selfish preoccupations.

Using smudge herbs before and after healing work is a wise practice. This can be extended into daily routine as well. It reminds you to release negativity and helps to clear it away. It reminds you to tend to the subtle levels of relationship with the world. You brush your hair and teeth, bathe, put on clean clothes—why not smudge too? As well, consider smudging your vehicle, especially before and during long journeys.

In medicine work, smudge herbs help maintain sacred spaces and ceremonial objects. Less obvious uses are to clear sleeping areas after fearful dreams, or to renew other spaces that have been sites of unhappiness, stagnant or cluttered mental energies, or trauma of any kind. Smudge after conflict, illness, accident, or depression. It aids in dissipating negative formations, thus clearing the air. It makes repetition of the same negativities less likely to occur.

You might consider smudging anything you want to keep free of tagged-on influences. I smudge such things as manuscripts, some of the letters and gifts I send or receive, offerings, the woodstove, hazardous tools such as chainsaws, and photographs of people or places I am doing medicine work for. This is in addition to the usual maintenance of altars and medicine objects. (It's a good thing I live near sage country!) This list gives some indication of smudging's versatility; it is not just for ceremonial occasion.

In the South is the Fire element. The maintenance here is your inner fire. This work, which includes attending to your chakras, can easily be accomplished before you rise in the morning and before you fall asleep at night. Spot-checks during the day keep you in touch with appropriate balances of energy. As with smudging, you also benefit from tending to your chakras before and after metaphysical work for others, or before participating in ceremony.

You can use inner light to maintain yourself in many ways. Light can be protective, energizing, revealing, or a medium of orientation. External light such as candles are useful in healing and clearing. A fire can be the altar for much of the South's maintenance practices.

Part of the South work means taking care of your sexual fire, too, and nurturing yourself with warmth, play, and friendship. Depletion of your fire puts you in a state where you are not energetic enough to help others, and your well-being becomes fragile. There is no virtue in becoming weakened through demands on your fire that are not countered by effective renewal. Some breathing, meditation, or martial arts techniques build inner fire. External sources of heat do not replace the necessity for cultivating the internal flame. You may have health imbalances interfering with your inner heat. Acupuncture and herbalism in particular help balance inner fire, and may be helpful in your maintenance. More physical exercise may also be called for.

Turning to the West, you find the medicine of Water. This element is incorporated into well-being's maintenance in a direct manner, through washing. Before and after working with someone, wash your hands, if not your whole body. Intuition will tell you how hot or cold the water needs to be. This has a cleansing and renewing effect. A practice I learned in midwifery—where you do a lot of handwashing—is to consciously release fear and confusion, letting them flow out through your hands and down the drain, with a prayer for their transformation.

Water has a tremendous capacity to refresh because of its elemental ties to emotions and its natural clearing qualities. You can remember this anytime you release some of your own fluid, such as urine, sweat, tears, or blood. It is apparent that there is an emotional release occurring when you cry, but you can let go of feelings at other times too, by sweating out your agitation, or peeing away what has been repressed, or using an occasion when blood flows to release old patterns.

For drawing out harmful influences or toxicities, use footbaths, handbaths, or full-body soaks in hot water to which equal parts (by weight, not volume) of baking soda and sea salt are dissolved.

Water maintenance includes what is needed to nurture emotional peace, and that often entails retreating periodically for solitude. Water may be part of this—camping by a river or lake, walking the ocean shore, or meditating beside a creek. It may be a retreat to a natural hot springs where you can relax in healing waters. Pre-ceremonial bathing is traditional, but your use of water as an element of spiritual practice need not be confined to formal situations. Almost any time a shift in emotions is needed, water can be the appropriate ally. It can move what seems stuck and dissolve what feels adherent.

The North's element is Stone or Earth. The primary maintenance practice associated with this is grounding. Connectedness is how manifestation moves. Grounding is connectedness to the Earth as an orientation for manifestation. It may be used to counteract psychic overload or high-energy spaciness, but that is not grounding's only application. It is a daily maintenance of awareness that nourishes, sustains, and aligns embodiment. It roots being and doing in a foundation of Earthly purpose.

This in no way separates you from celestial or divine purpose—

like the rooted, upreaching tree, you participate in what is beneath and what is above, and are in touch with resources from both. Grounding is being in touch with the beneath, with where you stand and how you dance in this life.

When you remember the sacred ordinariness of your connection with the Earth through the many ways of your interaction with it, your grounding is more naturally maintained. As with other elemental practices, special attention to grounding is important in relation to ceremony or medicine work. It helps you center and open yourself to what guides the work and gives it context on this Earth, connecting it to the powers of manifestation.

Individual stones can be maintenance allies, particularly obsidian or other stones whose natures strengthen and nourish you. In the North is also maintenance of the body—using food wisely, pacing your energy, and giving good care to your physical vessel. As a spiritual practitioner, you may not be giving enough attention to your own health. This is an area where practitioners can provide each other with reciprocal services—massage, healing, and expertise. North maintenance may include a change of scenery, a rest, or a shift of focus bringing more energy into and through the body.

Besides this round of elemental approaches to well-being, there are considerations in your intimate environment also, the main ones being your home and work spaces. Some aspects to look at are physical and metaphysical housekeeping, and how things are arranged.

All levels of housekeeping can be accessed and expressed through the physical. Of course, the more intentional you are about the metaphysical, the more effective physical efforts will be on those other planes. In general, physically cleaning your living and work spaces has an important and positive impact on the activities carried out in them.

Housekeeping is a renewal process, over and over (and over again!) bringing attention to active participation in the maintenance of well-being. If someone else does this work for you, vital aspects of maturity and participation remain undeveloped. Housekeeping can honor the giveaway of all that is part of your sheltering spaces and can make you more aware of what makes up those spaces. A result of this can be to make changes in what you have around you or in how things are arranged. Housekeeping is not only a cyclic process of renewal, it is an opportunity for awareness and change. For someone whose energies tend to be oriented in the upper chakras, housekeeping itself can bring balance or grounding.

You might view your home and workplace through the Oriental perspective of feng shui, or find inspiration from other traditional principles of arrangement. You may want to coordinate your maintenance tasks with moon or astrological phases, or other cycles that make sense to you.

New moons are regular cleaning and renewal times for me. I do major housework at those times, work that includes washing my stones, crystals, and shells as well as sweeping, dusting, and scrubbing the house. I check to see what needs change or rearrangement. The altar receives particular attention. Then I smudge everything with sage, followed by sweetgrass, and lastly take a shower and smudge myself and whoever else is around. The whole house lightens as this is done. It looks good, it smells good, it feels good. This kind of maintenance is internal as well as external—one reflects the other. The more consciously this is approached, the more it becomes an integrated facet of spiritual practice.

three

CEREMONY

Continuing with a medicine wheel perspective, the elements of ceremony can also be looked at in terms of the four Directions. This view is helpful for formulating your own ceremony, or when contemplating established forms.

East, being the realm of intention, is represented in the preparation and use of ceremonial offerings. These carry intention, becoming envoys of sacred purpose. The more clearly charged the offerings are, the stronger the sense of purpose within ceremony. Intention can be expressed through other means, but the use of offerings has lasted as a tradition because it extends commitment beyond mental levels. Intention begins on the inner plane and is ritualized, formalized, and manifested through offerings or similar vehicles.

East is the Direction of seeing and understanding, so the aspects of ceremony that are visually symbolic also belong to the East's influence. These can include the details of vestments or regalia, color themes, representative objects, and so on.

South's province is the altar. This is where personal relationship with the sacred is focused in ceremony. The component objects and their configuration, whether traditional or idiosyncratic, reflect personal alignment: they describe relationship. The altar is where worlds open to each other—a spiritual intersection in the universe. It is often where you place those things connecting you most directly with the powers you intend to access through ceremony.

South's capacity to connect is also present in the ways people relate to each other during these occasions. This includes both the protocols of the particular ceremonial form and spontaneous interactions.

The West's gift to ceremony is the movement of consciousness into nonordinary states. Fluidity of consciousness allows perception to traverse the realms, dissolving the sense of boundaries separating them. This fluidity facilitates the movement of manifestation from one level to another so that, for instance, a healing ceremony may actualize well-being through the physical plane. Power is conducted through the West's elemental medium like electricity is conducted through water.

The faculty of intuitive hearing—inner receptivity—is also part of the West. Hearing is a mechanism of acceptance, having its place in ceremony in the form of guidance and attunement, and in the hearing of invocation, song, prayer, or chant.

North is associated with physical structures, tools, patterns, and gestures in ceremony. It is the form itself. The structure may be a sweat lodge, a henge, a medicine wheel, a kiva, a dance ground, a circle chalked on the floor. It is a shaping of sacred space. It could conceivably be as vast as the cosmos or as subtle as the mind.

The tools of ceremony are consecrated objects serving to both orchestrate spiritual activity and focus spiritual power in differentiated forms. These tools may be elaborate or they may simply be what is at hand. Gesture and movement in ceremony is often stylized, repetitious, and reflective or initiative of inner movement. Dance is included in this.

Underlying all these North aspects is pattern. Each ceremony's pattern aligns it with a resonant field of energy. This is particularly powerful with a traditional form. Even the use of fragments of that form—songs, prayers, movements, structures—will to a certain extent activate the resonant effect. This may be especially noticeable when ceremony takes place in timeless places where awareness of those fields is not hindered by your surroundings.

Ceremony and ritual have become repopularized in alternative spirituality. Some of this is a search for replacing what many people miss in their lives after leaving the religion of their childhood. Some of it is a seeking back into pre-Christian roots of worship and magic. Some is a natural expression of relationship with the sacred.

Frequent in "open" ceremonies is a lack of clear group intent. Often the purpose appears to be just the act of raising energy, which is somewhat analogous to teenagers getting together to raise hell. What is being done with what is raised? What happens when you rouse things through invocation, and have no reason for doing so and no intelligent focus for those forces? Most of the time the results are just a hyping-up of the group, followed by frenzied dancing or emotional catharsis, after which people eat and drink and then go home to have bizarre dreams.

Other more worrisome results are when people get "out there" and need retrieval; or are left open to harm from the stimulated energies around them; or misdirect the power being raised through confusion of intention. All these can be reduced by having a clear, shared intention and a ceremonial process in which everyone can effectively participate.

Ceremonies whose purpose is to raise and (hopefully) make focused use of power are similar to fund-raising events: they use a gathering of people to magnetize certain resources that are earmarked for a cause. Another type of ceremony is coming together in order to align on a transcendent level of energy. This is what some drumming circles enact. Celebration, honoring, and worship are objectives of yet other kinds of ceremony, and still another category is ceremony for accessing information, knowledge, or aid through supernatural means.

No doubt there are more kinds of ceremonies than these, but this gives a view of how purpose, and thus procedure, vary. You may find your own practice mainly fitting one category, reflecting the focus of your relationship to Spirit. If your work is entirely unceremonious, you might consider whether a dimension of your spirituality is inhibited. Ceremony need not be formal or elaborate, but it does epitomize your respectful, attentive interaction with Spirit. It gives sacred context for enacting your work. Ceremony's components are meant to shift consciousness out of conventional modes. If skillfully used, these components orient and guide attention in accord with your ceremonial purpose. They give path and process for the movement of consciousness. For some people this is more necessary than for others, but it is especially useful in group situations. It also honors the gift of spiritual communion.

In some ways, ceremony is a performance art, but if it does not go beyond that, something is amiss. As a practitioner, it may help to think of conducting ceremony rather than leading it. A good conductor is a conduit facilitating the passage of energy, like a silver wire connecting an electrical outlet to a lamp. During the passage of current, wire and power are not separate, but the wire does not claim to own or be the power.

Access to current is not something to be careless about. Neither is it something to jealously guard, use selfishly, or feel superior about having. Some mediums conduct more easily than others—that is all. A silver wire will not be much use for shielding radioactivity, for example. Each person has his own talents. The wonderful capacity we are all born with is to grow and learn in whatever directions serve well-being.

Conducting can also be considered in its aspect of orchestrating. Each instrument has its notes to play in the symphony—its unique vibration to contribute. The conductor's role is not to make the music but to coordinate participation, to indicate pace and volume, to know the music so well that it is invoked through the connectedness and attention of the musicians. The conductor's absorption in the music may inspire the musicians. Another conductor's matter-of-fact competency may elicit confidence and calmness from the orchestra. However you look at it, and whatever your style, leading ceremony should not become the job of ego.

four

TIMING

In the North, the medicine of stone and ice and crystal give a feeling of held time. Their patterns move and change very slowly. In them is a quality of remembrance. Right timing is a teaching of the North. It applies to both inner and outer cycles of manifestation. Right timing is an attribute of wisdom: knowing when to speak or be silent, when to offer help or stand aside, when a task is most appropriately attempted, when to sympathize and when to laugh. Right action given wrong timing will do little good. Everything has its season.

In natural spirituality you learn much from attending to nature's cycles. From the timing of a fruiting tree to the gauging of a predator's leap, there is an intricate weaving of cyclic movement throughout the ecosystem. Each action is part of a seasonal web of interdependency.

An essential aspect of right timing is patience, and as patience grows so does wisdom. Wise timing is necessary in healing work, in counseling, in growing food, in ceremony, in childraising, and in most other activities of life. For the spiritual practitioner, a cultivation of patience will open the capacity for true service.

Regardless of where you live, tuning in to natural seasonal rhythms will help you find and be aided by resources prevalent at any given time. The same applies to the shorter rhythms of the moon. In this chapter, then, I offer some suggestions for ways to attune to seasonal energies.

IN SPRING:

- Focus on bird medicine. Work with whatever feathers you have collected. Meditate on bird-ness; renew your alliances. Pay attention to the birds around you—to their songs, flight patterns, and interactions. Set out nesting materials: clumps of shedded pet hair, small pieces of string, bits of natural cushion stuffing. Make nesting boxes. Plant trees or shrubs that are good sources of bird food or shelter.
- Focus on planting a garden, a new project, a new way of practice—something that will nourish the greater good.
- Focus on clearing. Smudge often. Sort through your belongings and give away what is not needed. Renew your surroundings. Move things, change things, lighten up. Clear stagnant patterns of emotion you have allowed yourself to cling to and identify with for too long. Sweep out the mental closet and formulate fresh intentions.
- Focus on dawn and morning energies. Pray or meditate early in the day. Focus on breath. Greet the light with gratitude. Walk outside and welcome the life emerging into spring's vitality. Let go of the night. Move outward.
- Focus on creativity. Cultivate your talents, invoke them from your fertile depths. Learn new skills, listen to teachings, open your mind. Awaken to participation in life.

IN SUMMER:

- Focus on alliance. Become more active, explore new levels, expand relationship.
- Focus on ego work that needs attending to. Face yourself honestly. Find out how to let individuality express itself naturally, unselfconsciously, without preoccupation.
- Focus on freeing desire from distorting emotions and beliefs. Work also with the medicine of sexuality and its relationship with desire. Find a path of reconnection with the sacredness of these energies, and align them with right relationship.

- Focus on chakra work. Spend time each day checking into the chakras and making necessary adjustments in the aura. Practice using different patterns of flow through the chakra system. Become sensitive to the habits of your energy.
- Focus on interaction. Raise the level of your socializing so that it reflects worthwhile modes of relationship. Clear negative patterns and establish positive ones.
- Focus on opening to happiness. Touch the Earth, smell and taste it. Feast your eyes on it; listen to its voice. Connect and allow connection. Unfold and stretch yourself to life's warmth. Play, laugh, have fun.

IN AUTUMN:

- Focus on sorting; focus on what needs release and what should be stored. Find your balance and what serves it. Pause and look at where you are, getting a sense of how to move in the coming cycle. Look at where you have been, and integrate the lessons derived. Take care of unfinished business.
- Focus on beauty. Tune in to life's song. Align with a natural rhythm that nurtures grace. Let your consciousness abide in beauty, move in beauty, reflect beauty, invoke beauty.
- Focus on evening energies. Make prayers of gratitude and good heart. Let go of anxieties and tension. Send awareness into the between places of transition, transmutation, and mystery. Open to larger possibilities. Tune in to subtle realms. Work with a fluidity of consciousness.
- Focus on deepening the heart. Expand your willingness to love, to be compassionate, to forgive, to let go, to nurture. Dissolve beliefs or boundaries that hold you away from the heart's strength. Express generosity. Learn to embrace without grasping. Free your griefs and let them flow toward healing.
- Focus on guidance and dreaming. Explore divination. Develop intuition and lucid dreaming. Get a clearer sense of relationship with guides and teachers.
- Focus on useful introspection. Perhaps go on a retreat or

arrange a time of solitude. Bring your spiritual practice to a new level of resource and power. Look within with intentions of release and movement. Proceed with wholeheartedness. Dispel shadows.

IN WINTER:

- Focus on renewal. Rest, move quietly, gestate vitality for spring. Nourish the body; nourish those around you. Learn to be still and peaceful. Move from your center, paying attention to what you are doing. Read, draw, cuddle, tell people you are glad they are alive. Tend to what needs fixing. Let go of judgments.
- Focus on plans. Design a house, think about what to put in the garden, make lists, invent a new livelihood, write a will, figure out a budget, incubate a dream.
- Focus on sharing. This is a season for giving: gifts that express appreciation, gifts that are the sharing of knowledge, skill, or craft. Elders give teachings, stories, memories, gifts of ancestry, perspective. Each person finds what can be shared, what adds another lighted strand to the communal web.
- Focus on patience. Learn the patience of waiting, of moving carefully, and accepting the moment. Learn the patience of stillness and of process. Learn to let things unfold and to do things meticulously. Learn to respect that each thing and each person has its own pace.
- Focus on roots. Tap into your ancestral current and what it has to teach, to give, and to ask of you. Honor family and all that supports you in this Earthly life. Strengthen your grounding. Become aware of the giveaway made each day to sustain your presence in the world. Make offerings of gratitude. Seek to be of service. Align with primordial purpose. Be like a buffalo.

One season opens to the next, an endless flow of rhythmic energy— change and motion, natural truths, the making possible of healing, realization, enlightenment, renewal. When you set yourself in congenial relationship with this flow, you experience its potential.

The wisdom of timing attunes to the larger matrix. The more in touch you are with the strands of cause and condition that surround situations, the more you can choose actions (or nonactions) commensurate with the best interests of the whole. Attuning to this larger context requires a far-reaching perspective. This capacity grows with experience, if you have patience and discernment.

Good timing can sometimes be instinctual, as with the leaping predator, but even successful instinct requires honing of other qualities. Instinctually wise timing is the mark of the good comedian, the natural athlete, and the intuitive healer, but wisdom, to move beyond a single application, takes a cultivation of wider awareness and commitment.

The I Ching centers on right timing. This is a t'ai chi perspective, a dance of force and receptivity, a finding of balance in motion. "Perseverance furthers," it will say. Or it may indicate the equivalent of "Chill out, don't push." Balance is not sameness; there are no easy rules for right choices. Each situation has its nuances, conditions, and factors that may confound ethics, morals, and logic. Knowing what to do and when is not something you can perfect. It is only another arena for learning and practice, for connection and perception.

The beauty of right timing can be appreciated when seeing the butterfly emerge just as its food source becomes available, or when hearing the youth's bat and ball intersect with a satisfying "whack!" or when the letter from a friend arrives on the day you are feeling so blue. There is much good timing in the world. It is part of our natural communalness, and as you become more in touch with that web, your own timing will come into synch.

five

SERVICE

The outward face of spirituality is service to community. The inward face is service to personal evolution. If the core of being and doing is aligned with whatever you name your ultimate Truth—Spirit, Mystery, Clear Mind, God—both these faces of spirituality can serve Truth's transcendent purpose. With that alignment, the two faces are one; without it, the two aspects may become estranged.

This chapter and the next specifically address the practitioner's role in service to community—the outward face of alignment with Spirit. The primary ways that metaphysical practitioners interact with community are through direct healing, counsel, spiritual mediation, divination, teaching, traditional expertise, and presence. Counsel will be discussed in the chapter following this one.

Direct healing may be through hands-on approaches, herbalism, aura work, prayer, shamanic intervention, or any combination of techniques and faith, as long as its basis is spiritual. To be a healer is to walk a path of transformative truth. Over and over that truth is affirmed through well-being's restoration. The healer's gift is to help reconnect awareness to well-being. The techniques used are not as important as the alignment that supports them.

A person does not have to be perfect in order to serve as a healer. The wounded or unhealed healer is participating in reconnection also, and applying what is learned in that process to serve others. That process teaches more than workable technique. It shapes attitudes, tempers egotism, and deepens compassion. It gives a grounding of experience, motivation for sharing, and credibility in that sharing. We heal together.

The qualities most essential in a healer are ones that increase with practice and commitment. Stamina is important. Healing is demanding work, bringing you face-to-face with the shadows. It requires a strength enabling you to respond when needed and to stay with the process as long as needed.

Compassion is vital, as are courage and a kind touch. A healer needs reliable access to spiritual resources and fearless skill in using them. Clear perception, good timing, and intuitive flexibility all help a healer respond effectively to each situation.

Healing is a mediation of one kind. Mediation itself is a separate category of service, mainly one of practitioners specializing in shamanism. Shamanic mediation involves acting as a spiritual go-between—communicating with spirits, obtaining information and help through nonordinary means, and performing medicine work bridging spiritual realms.

A mediator needs to be adept at moving through different states of consciousness. A healer acts as conduit, a mediator as messenger and translator. The qualities needed for mediation center around the ability to move into and operate effectively in altered states of consciousness. Part of this involves being on good terms with spirit guides and helpers. The practitioner must be able to journey without fear, know how to navigate nonordinary dimensions, and bring whatever information, power, or aid is needed from those precincts. This takes a unique combination of fluidity and stability.

Spiritual mediation is a service of maintaining relationship between the levels of causation and manifestation, and of harmonious interaction with the web of life. It maintains humans' positive participation in the matrix of the unseen world.

When defined as the use of an interface to access metaphysical insight, divination is another path of service. Commonly used interfaces are such things as tarot, crystals, oracles, runes, astrology, numerology, geomancy, dowsing, kinesiology, scrying, palmistry, and automatic writing. These can be utilized at many levels and for many different applications, not all of which are paths of reconnection or service.

Healing reconnects people with well-being. Mediation reconnects people with right relationship. Divination is a reconnection with intuitive guidance. This accessing of insight during divination should occur not only for the practitioner but also for the person seeking help. The practitioner acts as an experienced companion on the path, whose vision and understanding of the terrain are assets to be shared.

Besides these qualities, the divination practitioner needs to possess a particular depth of intuition and the capacity to set aside preconceptions and expectations. Divination requires observation and interpretation of symbols, patterns, and trends. It requires that the practitioner discern many threads and decipher the larger design they weave—to note detail and context and intuit their messages. This must be translated into useful communication so that the seeker participates by reconnecting with her own flow of guidance.

Reconnection with truth is the service of the teacher. Information, knowledge, and perspective are the tools of teaching, but the spiritual gift of it is an opening of access to truth. A good teacher does not tell people what to think or believe. Truth is what arises in the clarity of personal understanding or experience. It may happen in an "aha" moment as a teacher says something that suddenly enlightens, or it may emerge in gradual realizations, but it is not transferred like a parcel from teacher to listener. The truths accessed do not necessarily have to be Ultimate Truths in order to be valid or useful to the seeker. Consciousness operates on many levels, and needs truths for each of these stratas.

A good teacher offers what he or she knows not so that the student will know the same thing but so that the student will move through the door of his own house of discovery. Knowledge itself is not truth, but is a powerful key for expansion, exploration, understanding, and revelation.

A teacher needs the qualities of clear expression, effective transmission, and credible knowledge. Teaching is a cooperative activity: the student should not be a passive receptacle; the teacher should not assume superior assets. By invoking what is needed, the student moves the teacher's consciousness into new realizations as well. It is an interplay of minds, not a hierarchy of roles. Metaphysical teaching brings spiritual experience into the realm of understanding, spiritualizing the mind, aligning it with truth and with the capacity to communicate truth.

Traditional expertise and leadership is a category that overlaps others, but also includes cultural roles of ceremonial leadership, caretaker of sacred bundles and songs, keeper of cultural traditions, and a community resource in spiritual matters. This role is accorded a person by the community or by spiritual mentors—it is not a self-appointed function. Often it is connected to family lineage, or is transmitted by a teacher or predecessor or through acceptance of responsibility for sacred cultural objects or bodies of teachings. In general, it is more culturally linked than the other categories of service and more integrated with a particular community, tribe, or tradition. Such roles include Buddhist Rinpoches, Hindu gurus, African sangomas, and North American medicine people.

Some aspects of this work may be performed by practitioners who are not lineage holders or traditional leaders, though this sometimes enters hazy areas of modernization or cultural adaptations of traditional forms and practices. The role of spiritual leader is distinct in its relation to continuity and community recognition.

A facet of service that is both traditional and modern is that of heyoka or contrary. This is sometimes a phase or aspect of other categories of service. Contraries function as catalysts, disrupting individual and group patterns of complacency. This has great value for community, but what are the teachings in it for the person called to this role?

Most heyokas are people of power. Traditional cultures recognize that power needs a balance of humility or a strong context of service, so one of the primary teachings in the role of contrary is about ego.

In order for a person to usefully serve community and be an agent of Spirit, they must come to terms with self and Self. Heyoka medicine speaks both to the person with a lost sense of ego and to the one with a big sense of self. Either way, there is ego work to do, and contrary medicine brings this to the surface, compelling engagement. Heyoka was never a chosen role—it was always designated by Spirit through dream or vision—and this is still valid for today's spiritual practitioners. The path of power offers appropriate vehicles for understanding and movement at each stage of the journey. The beauty of this is that it always operates at both the individual and communal levels, demonstrating again and again that what the individual needs is never separate from the needs and good of the whole.

The last aspect of service categorized here is that of presence. A spiritual practitioner's presence in community should be an embodiment of honest, loving participation in life. This in no way means a practitioner is expected to be (or appear to be) an ideal person. It is commitment to good relationship through living your core beliefs. Living is a process, an experience in motion, of growing, learning, maturing. As a practitioner you try to live with compassion and goodwill. In doing this your presence serves as a reconnection to love, openness, and integrity; to bringing out the best in one another; to acceptance and forgiveness.

The qualities that a practitioner's presence embodies are very simple at their best, but they are not always easy to acheive. Ordinariness is a mark of mature practitioners. There is no flash and dazzle around them. The mature practitioner integrates spirituality into daily life so seamlessly that it demonstrates how natural and possible a life connected with Spirit can be. The adept does not need to show off, to gain followers, or to be above anyone else.

This practitioner asks for and allows help from others, encourages each light to shine, is part of community's dynamic of giving and receiving. This honors interdependency, generosity, caring, and kindness.

Other qualities that make presence a service are humor, the ability to communicate with all sorts of people, patience, honesty, respect for differences and sight beyond them, and helping people find common ground for healing and harmoniously living together. This is done not through instruction, but by living truth in a humble way, redirecting conflict to focus on common needs and cooperation.

One of the difficulties faced by spiritual practitioners in modern society is that healing and metaphysics are no longer at the center of society. Mainstream religions and medical systems have pushed primal spiritual approaches to the fringes, leaving many practitioners in isolated positions in regard to community. This sense of isolation is often reinforced by the practitioner's own temperament or way of relating.

There are several avenues of response to this problem. Some practitioners modify their practices to be more modern-seeming. This can take the form of changes in spiritual vocabulary, changes in personal presentation (an office, mainstream wardrobe, résumé, and so on), and outreach to related caregivers such as psychologists, clergy, physicians, and therapists.

Another type of response is to simply open communication with community. Self-acceptance is an important aspect of being able to succeed at this, as is acceptance of differences. If you use language that is not specialized or exclusive, adopt a non-adversarial attitude, and relate in a natural, unaffected manner, you have a better chance of finding grounds for mutual respect and cooperation.

Being a natural part of community rests first on seeing yourself as such, and thereby not limiting Spirit's range of influence. Spirit's work can move through all manner of possibilities. Staying connected to that primal current enables you to embody Spirit in whatever way best serves.

six

LISTENING

Wisdom is an attribute of the North, and certainly an appropriate one to invoke when offering the service of counsel. This chapter is entitled "Listening" instead of "Counsel" to emphasize that wisdom is better realized through receptivity than through thinking you have something to say. Counsel is the service of reconnecting to wisdom.

Deep listening is paying attention in a stillness of self. This attention has a center of peace and so is able to be receptive. Deep listening allows a person seeking counsel to speak wholly and uninhibitedly, and to open to wisdom. In deep listening, truth can be heard and shared. A practitioner may serve as healer, teacher, mediator, diviner, or spiritual presence without having to give counsel (though all these roles benefit from a capacity for listening), but a practitioner who is a spiritual (as opposed to psychological) counselor must have many of the qualities prerequisite for those other roles.

Listening denotes receptive, focused attention. The ears are part of this listening, but other senses come into use also. When a person comes to me for counsel, everything they do is expressive, is significant. My attention is engaged on many levels, connected through a center of quiet. I gather impressions from many sources: the person's clothing and appearance, his posture and movements, his aura and chakras, the observable state of his health and emotions, where he chooses to sit, his response to surroundings, and other such clues that give me a sense of what he is carrying inside.

As I listen, I hear not only the words but also the feelings, breath, spirit, and the things unsaid. I attend to the silence, and to gestures, changes in eye contact, and symbolism behind word choices. All these are noted, consciously or unconsciously, but without separation from the heart of deep listening. This is not a practice of intellectual observation or detached scrutiny; it is part of being with that person in complete attention.

Personal reactions rise and subside—they are not a focus. I keep my posture open and relaxed but centered in my own integrity; receptivity requires respectful attention, not indiscriminate empathizing. There are times when people vent negativity or give emphasis to ugly, traumatic experiences in graphic detail. Instead of either blocking these out or absorbing them into my consciousness, I often adjust my listening so that as the person speaks I make silent prayers transforming energies as they come forth. It does no one any good for ugliness, charged with fear and suffering, to indelibly imprint its images on first one memory and then another, reinforcing its evil. It is right that people should speak of these things, and be heard, but it serves healing more effectively to listen in prayer instead of becoming a vessel for negative images.

The beauty of deep listening is that you are not figuring out what you will say in return. You have no brand of therapy to apply and no performance to make. You listen deeply to the person seeking counsel, then you listen deeply to Spirit as it speaks. All the gathered impressions feed through your core alignment and encounter wisdom there. It is like handing a child to a mother aligned with caregiving. She will consciously and unconsciously receive the child's signals, and respond wisely to the baby's needs. This does not work if the mother's attention is distracted or if her alignment is skewed. Then she may miss the fact that the child is crying because of a banged knee, not because of bad temper, and that what is needed is first aid and comfort, not chastisement.

Giving counsel is different from giving advice. Counsel offers perspective without judgment or expectation. Besides listening, the resources of counsel are experience beyond ego concerns, clarity of discernment, ability to perceive patterns, compassion, connection to wisdom, and communication skills. Without listening, however, you are more teacher than counselor. Wisdom is gained, and shared, in listening.

When my mother was pregnant with me she dreamed of standing under a lighted lamppost with a little red-haired girl who was teaching her. All through life people have asked me for counsel, though I have often lived unwisely and sometimes self-destructively. Since childhood people have seemed to me to be like glass—easy to see within. The seeing was my teacher.

Sometimes it is a grace—to see is to know great beauty as well as pain. With the seeing I learned to listen deeply, because surface conversation with humans is usually a mask contradicting what is seen beneath, creating discrepancies. To be integrated, the seeing and listening require inner quiet, so that was learned too. In the quiet I began to find wisdom. This matures in conjunction with spiritual alignment.

Wisdom, in the North, has a quality of endurance, not sameness. It is mountainlike. It is rooted in truth, nourished by love, shared with humbleness. It cannot be owned, and it outlives us all. Children may have a wisdom of perception and elders a wisdom of experience, but it is not age that gives or takes wisdom. It is your willingness to listen to truth.

Counsel is not about having answers for people or recommending paths for them to follow. In natural spirituality, counsel addresses the core of what you believe and how you apply beliefs. It values the body's wisdom, the mind's wisdom, and the heart's wisdom, and integrates these, orienting them to Spirit and acting from that basis. Counsel, like healing, assumes transformation as a condition of reality.

To serve as a counselor you need to be able to simultaneously see others as the same and different from yourself. If you work only from your experience and what has applied to your own life, you will be helpful only on certain occasions. If you base counsel on the premise that no one is like you and seek a separate wisdom for each circumstance, you will likewise have limited effectiveness. The key is the awareness of interrelatedness, of pervasive consciousness and common patterns of experience, and also the ability to listen and see deeply enough to perceive the uniqueness of each dance with life.

All the variations come from a shared source. To perceive what is the same and what is different for each person requires that you let go of your neediness to have certain things be like or unlike you. This may sound simple but can be a challenging process. Individuals have a lot invested in self-images and in images of others. People often feel they are the only ones who are a certain way, yet worry about not being anything special. Your personal reactions in this realm of individuality can impair your ability to give good counsel. A related pitfall is to use counseling as a springboard for examining your own problems. The danger in this is projecting your process onto the person you are counseling.

People asking for counsel often are operating from a belief system not congruent with your own, but this should not be a barrier between you. Sometimes the respect of acceptance implicit in listening is all that a person needs. Counsel can reflect or redirect perspective. It can bring affirmation or revelation.

The practitioner who gives counsel needs to be trustworthy as well as wise—to keep confidentiality, to eschew bias and judgment, to be honest, and to respect vulnerability. There are some people who are good listeners but not good counselors. Some listeners use their abilities to draw others out in order to consciously or unconsciously gain advantage over that person. This may be a protective rather than passive-aggressive ploy, but regardless of that, it is not the kind of listening that serves wisdom and counsel. It does not even serve well-being.

Deep listening is a function of compassion, a way of being present with someone who is asking for perspective, connection, hearing, or insight. The wise counselor knows what serves each situation, whether it is to be a mirror, a door, a window, a chasm, a bridge, or a resource of knowledge and experience. Often it is stillness itself—the wisdom beyond words, the space in which we listen together—that gives the best counsel.

seven

Path

There comes a point when journeying on a spiritual path that the path is realized to simply be life itself. The path is not a road you follow but a journey you create with each breath. Accepting a body of teachings can give the illusion of having a marked road and a map to guide you, but these are only the stories of other journeyers.

It is like being in the forest. The spacing of trees and the land's contours guide your movement in a natural way, giving a sense of path. But it is your actual movement along that way that makes where you walk a path—in itself there is just the forest. Sometimes a predecessor will leave traces of her passage: a blaze on a tree, footprints, a campsite. Sometimes people pass the same way, but the path is still different each moment. Seasons change, the land changes, weather changes—what is there one day is not there the next, and what is noticed or experienced by one person is not what another finds on his journey.

The feeling of security or of progress that the notion of having a path gives is false comfort. All that can truly be yours is an alignment to Spirit. That will take you where it may, and the terrain might be pathless indeed.

Some practitioners go through what a friend of mine, knowledgeable about the Qabbalah, likens to an experience of the abyss. This seems to occur when you have accumulated extensive knowledge and skill and have reached a turning point in your work. Possession of knowledge can become a way of gripping life instead of moving through it. The occurrence of something outside understanding—an illness, a dream, a disturbing experience—may cause you to grasp for clarity, for an implicit teaching. What you are likely doing is grasping for control through understanding—a sense of knowing what is happening, and why, and what should be done in response so that you can get on course and be comfortable again.

Having knowledge and skill, you are armed for every occasion. By voluntarily disarming, yielding to the unknown, and divesting yourself of strategies, you begin to see a new way of using understanding. You see how not knowing can open you to truly experiencing your life and realizing more options, more paths to truth, and less grasping for control through knowledge.

To avoid the abyss, you can veer aside and continue your pattern of practice—perhaps with success, perhaps with stagnation. But to journey through the dark zone of the abyss you have to shed your luggage—your knowledge and carefully cultivated skills, your self-image, your professional expertise, your titles and credentials, your maps and plans, your spiritual career. You make an offering of these with respect, not rejection, and travel empty-handed into the abyss.

This is not an easy thing, and the choosing often seems made without definite consent. The abyss can be a place of challenge, a place of despair, fear, or strange, ghostly wandering. Vision cannot penetrate it. Your feet stumble; you become exhausted, dazed, estranged from others; or you feel you are going mad. Perspective is lost, truth is lost, connection is lost, there is no surety. Often there is a feeling of an initiatory void, of ego dissolving. Your objects become meaningless, your ceremonies feel empty, your altar seems the work of a stranger. You have little to say.

You keep moving, though without destination. Sometimes fear drives you, or sudden panic, or the habit of motion. Sometimes a friend reminds you that the abyss is spirit's choice of courage and commitment. Sometimes you move on a memory of faith: a distant star shines, resonates in your heart.

When you have let go of everything, seen what is in deepest

shadow and kept moving in your alignment with good, you know something that is true.

The gift of the abyss is a depth of yielding to self-knowing and what emerges from that. The more competent a practitioner you are, the easier it is to hide from the shadows. The more knowledge you have, the easier it is to avoid the unknown. The abyss is where the layers are stripped away to expose the bones, the core of who you are and what you are doing. There are no buffers there. If you are not ready to see the darkness, the abyss is not a place to venture.

Those who have traveled that land may find a listening within, a quieting of ego, a spiritual practice independent of externals, an alignment that has endured the death of self-image. Emerging from the abyss, you are no longer so easily intimidated by fear or insecurity or people's opinions or doubt. You do not expend so much energy hiding from yourself or others, shoring up infallibility or avoiding difficult situations.

The abyss reorganizes your priorities and exposes what is not essential. The journey through it may take years. It may shift your entire mode of practice and your sense of truth, or it may only bring greater depth to how you use what you have and know. In it you interface directly with the unknown; you relinquish control.

I remember coming from that dark, feeling as though familiar objects were being handled for the first time and going through the motions of ceremony or medicine work like a beginner. I made no attempt to return to my old ease with those things. I would find myself holding a rattle and having no song, or standing at my medicine wheel and having no words for prayer.

Slowly, what was appropriate became clear. I had changed, and the way I worked changed. It became stronger but also lost aspects that had been powerful and good. It was sometimes hard to accept that it was okay to let go of being good at something, or to know people's expectations and not fulfill them. It is a humbling experience, and an act of trust in Spirit. The commitment is to grow in understanding and love, not to be good at something. It sometimes seems a perverse process.

To be a useful practitioner you must welcome change, with or without the abyss. You cannot cling to a formulated path or imitate the assurance you imagine in other practitioners. The authenticity of your work is not challenged by change, it is nourished and vitalized by it. Your credibility as a practitioner is not invalidated by your personal struggles, it is informed and realized through them. Credibility rests on integrity, not on lack of difficulties.

There are several suggestions in relation to path that I think apply to all practitioners:

- Periodically rest from your practice. Go on retreat, or just take time off to gain perspective and renew yourself. Be open to change.
- Counsel with other practitioners. Compare notes, ask for input, share, listen. Take care of one another, teach each other, discuss issues, maintain connections, support, give feedback.
- Continue learning in order to move, not in order to have. Understand in order to take the next step, not to control where you stand.
- Question yourself periodically: Are you happy in what you are doing? Are the results of your work positive? Are you in a rut? Are your relationships good? Are your priorities aligned with Spirit? Are you real in your work? Is your work real in you?

The focus of your practice may shift as your work unfolds. You may express it in many different forms at various times in your journey. If guidance is clear it does not matter what the form is—the necessary experiences will emerge and the right service will be fulfilled. The North is spirit embodied in community. Your part in that is wisdom's path of expression. If you are willing to let your light shine, it will find its venue.

Through most of my adult life I was given specific guidance. "Be a midwife" came clear as a bell one day, before I had ever met a midwife. The herb business started the same way, as did the medicine work. I became used to definite guidance, and then it was gone. It still came within the details of medicine work, but not as an answer to "What next?" "Next" disappeared. There was only now.

It was disconcerting. Do I teach? Do I conduct ceremonies? Do I learn a profession? Don't things take some planning? How do I move without direction? It was one of those experiences of relinquishing something I was good at: knowing what's next. What it left is now-ness. In now-ness is an imperative of self-acceptance and acceptance of life. "You are here"—the arrow on the diagram nails your reality to the spot. It can be a claustrophobic moment. You can feel trapped and freak out, or accept it and discover how free this makes you. (Or you can try to project yourself elsewhere and thus live in illusion, out of synch with your true opportunities.)

When you learn to be with now-ness, guidance becomes an "And now" experience, rather than "What next?" In being fully present, you serve more fully and experience the gifts and teachings of what you do. With self-acceptance you participate with an open heart, a certainty that you belong in beauty, in sacred awareness of being. Now-ness is where all participation begins and ends and is renewed in each turning of the wheel. Now-ness is the path and the destination, and so you are always and already here.

Building a sweat lodge in autumn,
two of us dig, two cut saplings.
Tobacco on the Earth
and sage in the smudge bowl;
sun on embered leaves, the lake
ripples, ripples like a harp.
Earthworms in each turning
of the spade; we dig with care
into this harvest day.
Woven willow, our inverted nest,
the weaving a dance of four.
Heyoka child darts between saplings
and legs—can I tie it now?
Stones gathered and washed,
admired amid jokes about fire tenders;
stories remembered, released
like bright leaves.
We tell each other—you bring
buckets, and food for after;
I'll remember a fork for the rocks
and birch bark for the fire.
We'll need lots of coverings for
the lodge—it will be a good sweat.

PART FIVE

Earth

SWEAT LODGE

This chapter begins with a disclaimer. In more than a decade of working with the sweat lodge as a ceremonial leader, there have been many people interested in receiving instruction on how to conduct sweats. The one person to whom I have given instruction did not ask, but is suitable for that work. In writing about sweat lodge I am describing something that I recommend others do not undertake without proper calling and instruction. You cannot learn to be a sweat lodge leader from a book, anymore than you can learn shamanism from a book. It usually takes long-term commitment, a suitable nature, spiritual guidance and support, and teachings transmitted by an adept, experienced practitioner.

So why write about it? There is no ceremony that is the equivalent of sweat lodge. The teachings derived from conducting it are, however, applicable to many other ceremonial or healing (or life) situations. The sweat lodge is both unique and archetypal, as is childbirth, and—like childbirth—is something I have some experience with. In writing about sweat lodge I hope to share perspectives of practice that can be used in many contexts.

The disclaimer is this: The following should not be construed as instruction or encouragement for leading sweat lodges. It is my belief that this ceremonial form requires clear calling and in-person training to be conducted safely and competently. Further, what is presented here comes from my own experiences, and is not reflective of any particular Native American tradition.

My original experience with sweat lodge was with a Native medicine man in Michigan who was my spiritual mentor for some years. I have since associated with other Native practitioners, and have some small knowledge of various traditions, but what is presented in this book is from my own evolution with this ceremonial form. I am a Caucasian woman of Scottish descent; on the occasions when I have conducted sweats with Native people in attendance, there has not been negative reaction, and the ceremonial leaders I have associated with have been supportive of this work. So as far as I can ascertain, my way of conducting sweats is not at odds with Native practices. It is similar to how my mentor led sweats.

The sweat lodge and its many variations is an ancient, almost universal form of ceremonial cleansing and renewal. Its power moves through a primal, elemental process of transformation. The lodge is a timeless, sacred space where all worlds meet and all realms can be touched. It is a place of healing and truth, and of prayer-making for the well-being of all. It is a crucible where you learn to let go, a cauldron of rebirth, the womb where you find new beginnings if you have the heart to release the past. It is an old, old process, and the spirits of the lodge have been invoked many thousands of times over the centuries. Let us move through this ceremony as it has unfolded in my experience.

It is autumn. Leaves swirl as we choose a site for the lodge. What is needed is a clear space—no overhanging trees to be threatened by the fire—and level ground. We find a good spot with a hill nearby, sheltering the site from wind. The fire will be large, and the safety of the land is a paramount consideration.

We sit, communing with this place, and make prayers with offerings of tobacco, asking for blessings, for acceptance of our presence here. The group of participants smudges, then divides the tasks to be done: firewood split and stacked, kindling made, birchbark collected for starting the fire. A few people go off to cut saplings for the lodge frame, remembering to take tobacco for offerings to the trees.

Someone smudges the tools and the ceremonial area and begins digging a fire pit; tobacco is laid down for that too. Others haul water in jugs and collect stones. "Cantaloupe size or a bit bigger," they are told.

"Don't get them from anywhere wet or they'll explode in the fire, or worse yet, in the lodge. And don't forget to put tobacco down."

I pace off the space for the lodge. Someone makes a prayer and starts digging a rock pit near the center of where the lodge will stand, heaping dirt into a mound in front of where the door will be. It will be an East-facing lodge. The Earthen mound becomes an altar—hands pat it reverently into shape.

Lodge coverings are piled to one side of the work area, and other supplies are collected: a water bucket, cedar boughs for sitting on in the lodge, twine for securing the lodge saplings together. By this time the sapling cutters have returned, the fire and rock pits are dug, and we are ready to put up the lodge.

The doors are formed first. Two saplings spaced a few feet apart in the East and two more in the West are planted in the Earth—with sage at the bottom of the holes—and slowly, slowly bent across the center of the circle, joining to make a waist-high double arch. "Looks kind of low" someone comments.

"Don't worry," I say, "It will spring up a bit as we work." When finished the lodge will be about four feet high at center. The two South and the two North saplings are planted next, arched over, and tied. With these four Directional doors made, we complete the upside-down basket shape by arching the cross-quarter saplings over the middle in an X. Several long, flexible saplings circle the sides of the lodge parallel to the ground and are tied to the uprights. The web of willow is delicate-looking but quite sturdy.

We dress the lodge in blankets. The huge pile of blankets quickly dwindles as several layers are applied to block out all light. The canvas tarp goes on last. Cedar boughs are spread inside and on the altar mound, and the door flap to the lodge is left open.

With all the different tasks involved in lodge-building, you would think it would be accomplished easier with a large group of participants, but unless the group is experienced, it is usually simpler to build a lodge with only one or two helpers. With a large, inexperienced group, each task needs supervision and sometimes redoing. You hear questions such as: "How deep should the rock pit be?" "Are these saplings long enough? thin enough?" "Which blankets go over the door?" "Is the fire pit too small?" "How do you make holes for the saplings?" Snap! "Oh no, I bent it too fast." "Is this enough firewood?" "Will sandstone be okay?" and so on.

The sweat lodge ceremony uses a great amount of resource. This is one reason why it is good to have an established, maintained lodge, rather than rebuilding one for each sweat. There is tremendous giveaway made by the land: firewood, stones, saplings, boughs, bark, water, all used in abundance, and some cannot be reused—even basalt stones crumble after a few times through the fire. It is a reminder that this is not a ceremony to undertake without meaningful, wholehearted intention and participation.

In the late afternoon, as the lodge area is cleared of tools and unnecessary items, some people find quiet places of retreat in order to make tobacco ties to hang inside the lodge. Others rest, sipping water or juice in preparation for the heat to come. Everyone has fasted since at least noon.

The fire tender works alone, laying four base logs East to West and four North to South, stacking the stones I have selected and smudged—fourteen stones this time—on this platform of logs, then making a pyramid of wood around and over the stones. He leans cedar kindling against all four sides, clustering birchbark at the center of each so the fire can be lit in all four Directions.

The wind fades during the afternoon, and stillness is on the land as the sun begins to set. Anticipation stirs its own breeze through the group at the lodge. At my nod the fire tender takes tobacco from the pouch I had given him in asking for his service, and makes a prayer. The group is silent as he lights the birchbark in each Direction. The fire crackles, blazing to life as the sun dips below the hills. People settle onto log rounds and on the grass around the fire, gazing into the flames with the age-old fascination humans have with this element. The fire tender is the only person who crosses between the lodge and the fire; it is all one unit—the fire, altar, and lodge.

As leader, my work with the sweat began when I accepted tobacco in request for this ceremony some weeks before. Some of the tobacco is used in preparatory prayer, some in making the lodge. What is left I set on the East slope of the altar mound, available for anyone's use in making prayers.

I arrange medicine objects on top of the mound, leaving the sides bare for people's special objects or offerings. I set out the antlers used for guiding heated stones inside the lodge, and my rattle, smudge materials, and the carved wooden dipper another medicine person gifted me with.

I fill the water bucket, smudge the lodge, and walk the periphery of the ceremonial area with my rattle, praying and strengthening the integrity of our sacred space. Those who have made tobacco ties hang them in the lodge. Everything is done carefully, respectfully, and with deference to the sweat's leader. The fire tender adds wood to the blaze, tucks a stone deeper into the coals with his fork, ties a bandana around his forehead to keep sweat from his eyes. Someone offers him the water jug.

Superficial chatter is discouraged. I answer people's questions, speaking what I know of the ceremony's traditions—the significance of certain aspects of the form. Someone begins drumming softly, others sing. For a while after that there is silence except for the voice of the fire.

As the moon rises in a clear turquoise sky, the rocks heat to the core, becoming bright orange in their cradle of coals. I give notice that if anyone needs to empty their bladder, now is the time to do it. I ask the fire tender for a live coal, and he expertly flips one out of the fire and into the smudge bowl. I pile sage on top and hand the bowl and feather for fanning to someone experienced with smudging. After fanning the smoke over me, this person makes the rounds, smudging each participant thoroughly, including the fire tender and his fork.

People are in various states of dress and undress. Some wear loose clothing, others are naked under towel wraps. I make a final murmured prayer at the fire for the well-being of the people in the ceremony. I pray for Spirit to move through me and guide me in this service, and for right relationship with this ceremonial form. The fire takes the tobacco—it flares and is gone. Swathed in my towel I circle the fire and enter the lodge, uttering "All my relations" as I bend low to pass that threshold.

The lodge is cool within, another world. I circle the rock pit and arrive at my place in the Northeast, beside the door. The ground is cold beneath the cedar boughs. There is a feeling of home in the familiarity of this space, and also a sense of mystery, of unknown. Each sweat is the same and different. I feel the sapling against my back, and I greet the lodge, center myself, make a quiet prayer, let go of all but this place, this service.

The rattle and dipper are beside me. A braid of sweetgrass is tucked over a nearby sapling. I lean into the doorway to invite the people to enter. As each one crawls through the opening he or she circles clockwise, filling the lodge. Many of them murmur "All my relations" as they pass within. There are a few moments of towel-arranging and deciding what limbs go where as people settle themselves in the snug space. I feel their anxiety and alertness. It is good—it helps them be ready, be focused, forget ordinary preoccupations.

The fire tender hands me the antlers from the mound. "Seven stones," I tell him. I pass the sweetgrass to the person sitting on the other side of the doorway. As each stone is brought in, it is brushed with sweetgrass. The first seven stones are greeted and arranged in the center and six Directions. The first round of rock work is hard labor for the fire tender. The fire is at its hottest, though the flames have been allowed to die down, and it is blistering work fishing the stones out of the fierce coals. After making sure they are clean of ash, the fire tender carries each one balanced on the fork, and passes them carefully, carefully into the dark lodge.

As the laden fork passes in front of me, I grasp its handle with one hand, then use the antlers to guide the stone into place in the rock pit. The people marvel at each stone—how it sparkles and glows, casting light and heat. It is alive. The seventh stone in place, the fire tender hands in the water bucket, sets the antlers back on the mound, and drops the door coverings, closing us in.

Silence. Taut silence. The stones glow ferociously, beautifully. I ladle seven small dippers of water on the stones, one on each. Steam spits and explodes from the bright surfaces, mottled now from the water. The lodge is instantly hot, humid, charged with the energy of elements in their sudden transformations.

I breathe in the heat, feel its waves wash over me; I raise the rattle and begin the welcoming song. Those who know it join in after a bit, their voices uncertain at first, then stronger. The first prayer is in gratitude for the giveaway of the trees and the stones; for the service of the fire tender; for those who look after the people's children while parents sweat; for the presence of the spirits; for the tobacco, sage, and sweetgrass; for the fire, water, and air; and for the opportunity to participate in this sacred ceremony.

The second prayer greets and welcomes the East and its medicine, and the sacred beings of the East. After this prayer I ladle water on the stones, and pass the rattle across the doorway to the person sitting there. Steam fills the lodge. It feels good. Sweat runs freely down my body. I am glad to be here.

Part of my awareness constantly monitors the well-being of the people in the lodge. It is like keeping a finger on many pulses. I sense mental states, emotional tides, physical reactions, and movement in and out of transcendent consciousness. Occasionally there will be a sudden gap somewhere in the circle and I will know I have "lost" someone—they have gone out-of-body or spaced off somewhere, or perhaps shut down. This can usually be caught before it has gone too far. It is not something I ignore. With rare exception it is better for people to be present with themselves in the sweat lodge. I differentiate between transcendent states and "going away" or shutting down. I also see a difference between channeling and attuning to spirit presences, and do not encourage the former.

If someone is "lost" I can retrieve them, usually vocally, without disrupting the flow of ceremony. If they seem alright where they are, I will sometimes let them be until the end of the round. This monitoring is important, because people often will not speak up about what is happening with them for fear of violating some protocol or drawing unwanted attention. They can get into trouble—physically, emotionally, or psychically—and suffer to (or past) their breaking point without alerting anyone to their difficulties. The sweat lodge is completely dark, so you cannot rely on visual clues to let you know how people are doing. You have to be attentive in other ways. Crisis is not unusual in the sweat lodge, where conditions of heat, darkness, humidity, close quarters, and ceremonial intensity cut through superficial boundaries and facades. The elemental nature of the sweat brings out primal feelings, primal states of awareness. People lose their grip on pretension, and thereby find themselves. It can precipitate crisis, or it can be a tremendous relief. The leader must be able to respond calmly and effectively to crisis in a way that serves the whole group and is appropriate to this ceremony.

As the first round of the sweat unfolds, each person has a turn with the rattle, and makes a prayer or offers a song. After each, water is ladled on the stones—hissing; billowing steam; purifying the prayers, the people, the lodge. People moan, exclaim, sigh, shift their slippery bodies, suffer, and rejoice.

The rattle comes again to me, and I make a prayer and sing an Eagle song to close the round. "Door!" I call, and the fire tender lifts the blankets, steam rolling out the opening and cool, dry air drifting in like a saving grace. A water jug appears in the door and is handed around. It is as though no one has ever drank before—they are realizing how vital, how wonderful water tastes and feels. Their gratitude is immense and sincere: The cool air! The cool water! It is all anyone could ask for. They are humble and real in their gladness.

I check in with people who were struggling in some way during the first round. "Are you okay? Would you like to have a bit of sage? It's alright to put your head down if you're feeling overcome with the heat."

The water jug makes the round again. I offer suggestions to those having difficulties, and urge them to speak up when they need help. An important aspect of the sweat is the mutual support and trust that can be expressed. I ask for two more stones from the fire, then the door flap is lowered and the South round begins.

In earlier years I was a stricter leader. As time went by I became more flexible in ways that do not violate the integrity of the medicine as I know it. This situational flexibility helps those who might otherwise bail out partway through the ceremony. Two operative aspects I maintain are that people stay inside the lodge between rounds, and anyone deciding to depart the lodge partway through the ceremony cannot reenter. Some leaders conduct sweats differently, of course. I have no objection to people lying down (if they can find room), being naked or clothed, or shifting seating positions with someone else if necessary. A woman with only one lung asked if she could bring her asthma inhaler into the lodge; I gave clearance for that too.

The rounds are not always dedicated to the four Directions. The lodge is not always East-facing. Sometimes I receive spirit guidance to do things in a specific way, particularly with sweats that are requested for healing. The number of stones used varies; prayers and songs vary. Sometimes I do silent rounds, especially if people seem too performance-oriented; sometimes I do rounds in which everyone prays aloud simultaneously. Sometimes I do pipe sweats, particularly for vision-questers. These more closely follow the traditions I have been given.

The heat is the element that makes the sweat lodge the transformational ceremony it is. I work with the stones in whatever way they call for. Some sweats turn out milder or more scorching than others, but that is the will of Spirit moving through the stones, not of this leader.

The South round this night is relatively brief, but fierce. The new stones are like warriors proud in their radiance. The prayers express courage, commitment, and concern for loved ones. People pray for healing of relationships throughout the web of life. The rattle shakes vigorously as a snake's tail. The songs are strong. The round ends with water dancing into steam off the fresh stones, and my shout of "Door!" brings the fire tender with merciful quickness to the lodge.

This time people make free with the water that is passed in, pouring it over crisped hair, gasping when its cold shocks their steaming skin. No one is worried about how they look at this point. Towels are sodden. Bodies prop against each other with no more sexuality than children. "You okay?" I ask people. They breathe deeply and nod. "One more stone," I tell the fire tender. He brings a large one. Someone makes a dazed sound, someone else laughs. I wait for quiet, a return of focus. The door flap closes and the West round commences.

I pray. The rattle passes. There are spirit presences. I feel them come and go throughout the ceremony. Totem spirits, ancestor spirits, sacred beings of the land. Some I recognize, some not. I acknowledge them, attune to them; occasionally I see lights sparking the air—blue, sometimes purple or green. After the sweat I will ask the fire tender what was seen and heard outside. I keep one finger on the pulse of the spirits, one on the pulse of the people. The ceremony manifests through these balances, the worlds meeting. "Let us move in a sacred way," I pray, aligning with beauty and healing, with right relationship.

The heat feels stifling; my attention wavers. My heart is laboring, my back hurts, and the person beside me has his knee in my hip. My hair is too hot to touch, and so is the sapling I would like to lean against. The discipline of experience gently pushes all this aside. I straighten my back, move the energy through, surrender to the heat. I listen to the prayers, extending strength to those who need it.

The round is long—there are tears and slow, sometimes anguished prayers. They are slow but real, no more pretty speeches. They are heart prayers. The steam has penetrated everything. At the end of the round it billows through the door and the fire tender stands aside to let it pass.

The last stones are welcomed in, leaving two in the fire. They are received stoically, with tired awe. The sweetgrass brushes them and blesses the lodge with its fragrance. The water jug makes a last pass and is removed. The door flap lowers once more.

The North round calls up deep resource, moving with steady purpose like a buffalo. People are no longer worried about making it through. The prayers include many for friends, for people homeless, people imprisoned, people in war-torn places. The prayers remember the needs of the Earth's creatures, the rooted beings, the salmon, the endangered ones. The prayers address the Mystery, the Great Spirit, the Source. People try not to leave anything out, not to forget anything. They are relieved that the sweat is almost over, but realizing what that means.

In listening to the prayers, I use the steam to help them move and be empowered by this ceremony. Sometimes the prayers are not well presented—their energies or wording triggers a caution mechanism, and I use the steam differently then, to purify and transform the prayer, if necessary adding quiet words of my own to modify those energies. The sweat lodge is not a place for using words carelessly. It is too highly charged and too open to the realms of manifestation. Some sweat leaders do not let others pray during the ceremony at all.

The rattle comes again into my hands and I make a final North prayer, then one to the Earth, to the Sky, and to the Great Mystery. I express gratitude to all who helped us in the ceremony, in all realms, and ask that only good come from what was enacted. I end with a Lakota prayer given me to use. Water sizzles a last time on cooling stones, gurgling among the rocks at the bottom of the pile. The door flap is flung back, and after a few minutes of sitting in an emptied-out state of peace, the people crawl out one by one, easing past my place by the door and honoring "All my relations" as they pass into the moonlit night outside.

The fire is low—the fire tender has timed things so there is light and warmth but not a wasting of wood. The tobacco ties are taken out and burned along with the cedar boughs. People begin to converse gently, genuinely. I dress, and pack my medicine objects. People retrieve what is theirs from the altar mound. When everyone is ready, the fire is extinguished and we walk together to the house where food awaits. In the morning I will come back to tend to the ceremonial area. It is done.

Several aspects of ceremonial leadership are emphasized in conducting sweats. One is the act of leadership itself, which in this kind of ceremony is a role beyond that of facilitator. It is old fashioned in that regard, but appropriately so. The nature of the form asks that participants let go of boundaries and securities and beliefs, and be in a state of trust and acceptance. No matter how many times you sweat, you always enter the unknown at some point. The leader does not take control of this anymore than a midwife controls birth or has the baby for someone. Having a leader allows participants to experience that state of trust and acceptance, of being present with the unknown and with self in a sacred context.

A good leader is in touch with balances of safety and transcendence, knows the differences between habits of comfort (both physical and emotional) and true well-being. The leader is not interested in conducting an emotional drama or in creating an exercise in consciousness alteration. The point is not to get high, to have a group bonding experience, to conduct therapy, or to see who can endure the longest or get the furthest "out there." All these objectives are far easier to accomplish than the true experience of sweat lodge, which is healing, renewal, and alignment to the good of all. The leader needs to guide and maintain that focus, and invoke the forces that actualize that purpose.

The deference given the leader is respect for the process enacted through the sweat. The deference strengthens that process—it is not a giving away of power or an abdication of full participation. The leader knows this. He or she does not make personal prayers during the ceremony, does not lie down when it gets hot, does not become absorbed in private struggles or manipulate conditions to suit personal needs. The role of the leader is to be of service to Spirit and to be a presence aligned with the greater matrix.

Other sorts of ceremonies may not need leaders, or may be conducive to rotations of leadership. Shared responsibility is a positive thing, as it is a shift away from hierarchy. If ceremonial leadership becomes linked to issues of ego and power-over, it ceases to serve spiritual purpose. It could be compared to gender issues: To move away from oppression many women choose to move away from men. Similarly, to shift from hierarchy and egotism, many people have shifted away from having ceremonial leaders. In both cases there is a loss of what can be healed through coming into right relationship with each other and with self. Meeting challenges and seeing beneath them to the core of what is needed is a way of becoming whole. This is part of Earth's teachings.

I go upon the mountain,
upon the sacred ground
where stone, sand, and pine
speak their peace in detail
and completeness.
I go upon the mountain,
upon her steep side
with rough breath I climb,
meeting the heat and
the hidden call of birds
against the sky.
At dawn I go upon the
mountain, I go alone
with no offering to
pour upon the sand.

PART SIX

Sky

VISION-SEEKING

The disclaimer in the previous chapter applies to this one as well. The vision quest ceremony is an occasion where experienced guidance can make a world of difference. Again, the ground covered here will be toward a practitioner's perspective of service to the medicine that supports the seeker. Again, what is presented here is not necessarily traditional to Native ways of working with this form.

The teachings of sweat lodge leading are about conducting ceremony in right relationship with Spirit, with the people, and with self. The focus of vision quest support centers on wise counsel, and on maintenance of sacred space over extended time and distance.

As with sweats, the work begins with formal request. The answer to this request comes from inquiry into the practitioner's capacity to carry out this service, the seeker's capacity to productively engage in this ceremony, and the spiritual rightness of enacting this ceremony at a particular time.

There needs to be some concurrence about what vision-questing means to both seeker and supporter, and what expectations there are of each other. Sometimes it becomes apparent that another form of introspective solitude is more suitable for the seeker, and it is better to suggest this than to overly contort a traditional form to meet individual, modern needs. The cachet of vision-questing may be more appealing than that of camping or going on a retreat or just giving more time to prayer and contemplation, but if someone wants ceremonial support for a vision quest they should be prepared for what that particular form entails.

As with sweat lodge, situational flexibility is appropriate, loss of meaningful integrity is not. The adept practitioner perceives what furthers well-being and what negates the purpose and power of the form used. It's a little like going to a foreign country: If your intent is to stay in a Holiday Inn, eat American food, hang around with American people, and view a few historical sites from a tour bus window, what's the point? Is it only to say you've been there?

Two primary aspects of vision-seeking are removing yourself from ordinary surroundings and preoccupations and humbly opening to fulfillment of spiritual intention. How does the practitioner support this process? Support begins in the preparation period, when the seeker articulates his intentions and begins to discover what will facilitate their fulfillment. The practitioner, through questioning and offering perspective, helps the seeker look deeply into his intentions to see what initiates and surrounds them.

During the preparation period, which spans six months to one year, the seeker works through issues that may impede her quest time's focus. He does this through introspection, counsel, changes that spiritualize his life, and through implementing whatever protocols are particular to the form of vision quest he is entering into.

These protocols often include abstinences of some sort, the making of prayer ties or something similar, and the offering of tobacco and gifts to his supporters. Another aspect of preparation is the readiness to fast, and to be out in the elements and wilderness. Depending on previous experience, this can be a major challenge in itself.

The last consideration of this period is the seeker's rearrangement of life in order to make space for this ceremony to take place and be honored. This is an important realization of priority, and of letting go of the patterns of the past so that life can open to new directions. This is a severance of momentum and the influence of what is familiar. During this preparation time the practitioner listens and offers expertise. As with sweat lodge, deference is given the practitioner's role, but it is understood that this is a position of service and support, hopefully given through a wisdom of experience, knowledge, and calling.

The practitioner is also preparing—making prayers, attuning to the gathering energies, beginning to create a sense of sacred space, and becoming sensitive to the seeker's energy. This sensitivity helps the practitioner stay in contact with the seeker's state of being.

It is usual for the seeker to formally ask three or more elders to pray for him during the quest time, and this harmonizes with the work of the practitioner, providing a level of continuity with community that balances severance at other levels. It marks a shift of relationship with community, expressing the seeker's spiritual commitment. These supporters, or others, may attend the sweat lodge that usually begins the quest itself.

In viewing a practitioner's work from this point, let us move into a context of experience.

It is spring—the snows have not long departed the mountaintops. Early flowers push past the dried, brown stems of last year's growth. The pink of wild current blossoms softens the scenery's ruggedness: the rain-dark trunks of old-growth fir and cedar, the rocks rising from riverbanks that guide the Grey Wolf's swift, cold flow.

The seeker is in his chosen place, perhaps three miles from the clear-cut where I am camped. Over the years I have watched this place endeavor to reclaim itself: briars, thorns, and thistle taking over the ravaged earth, twining the tables of huge stumps, roots grasping the soil that otherwise is carried in runnels of silt downslope to the once salmon-filled river. A single tall fir, its trunk scorched and gouged by logging equipment, bleeds a slow weep of sap. This tree stands at the verge of this huge, unnatural meadow, surrounded by the watchful wilderness—river and forest and cool mountains. I am witness here, and though I live some miles away, I am no less dependent on its vitality than the deer, the thrushes, and the bears.

As my helper sets up camp I build a medicine wheel out of what is found around our site: stones, flowers, a raven feather, a fir cone. Whenever I pray at this wheel, or at the fire we keep continuous during the quest, I will use tobacco given by the seeker, and the unlit pipe I filled during the sweat.

The day is overcast and the wheel's stones are chill to the touch. After the initial prayers I help make camp, then sit in the afternoon quiet listening to the ravens, watching the juncos move busily from bush to bush. A flock of kinglets follows them. The river's voice is ever present. Clouds rest on the mountain's slopes, mingling with mist from the river. The forest has no spaces—mist fills the gaps between trees and jewels their mosses. I think of the quester on his ledge above the river.

Often, the first day is a time for quieting the mind. The ordinary pace and preoccupation of life ceases, and the quester is immobilized in a stillness that may echo with sudden doubt and agitation, with no outlet for darting thoughts. On the first day I orient prayer to the East, the place of mind, and call for the spirits of the East to help the quester deal with his thoughts, to find eaglelike perspective, to use his breath in prayer and centering.

A mind unused to such stillness around it will cast up formation after formation of distracting anxieties: "What if I don't have a vision? What if I do have a vision? Will I be able to last three whole days and nights here? Maybe I should have picked a better spot, a different time. I wonder if a bear will come. I wish I could have brought a journal. Maybe I shouldn't be doing this while so much is going on at work. I hope Susan remembers to order propane—we're almost out. Will she be able to move the tank alone? Maybe I should have worn wool pants instead of blue jeans. It looks like it will rain the whole time I'm here. Maybe the spirits want me to go home now . . ."

As thoughts skitter, drawing the seeker inexorably away from being present and in sacred alignment, there is need to disengage from this activity and bring the mind into synch with the harmony around it. The questing place is an embodiment of harmony—a place to be present with reality. As the seeker's attention comes to rest on what is there and knows it as a sacred space, the mind finds some peace. It remembers the quest's purpose; it focuses on prayer, and on being aware.

At my campsite the sun is setting, a dimming behind clouds that becomes complete as the bulk of the mountains gives us an early dusk, taking the light before we have finished cooking our evening meal. With the sunset I pray at the wheel, as I will with each dawn, noon, sunset, and late night. My helper puts tobacco in the fire with a prayer of her own, and dinner is ready when I finish at the wheel.

We eat in the tent—there is a misting rain. The fire is well banked with logs and has a deep bed of orange coals. It is a soft evening for all its damp, the clouds holding the Earth's warmth close to the ground. I sense vegetation growing as rain soaks into the forest floor. The ancient forest has seen thousands and thousands of these rains; it is an old partnership. The quester sits amid these elements—rain, soil, mist, the fire of life embered but steady within.

Night deepens and the rain slacks off. A breeze stirs the fir needles, the flame of our fire, the river mist. We venture out to breathe the spring-fertile air. I hear rustling in the tangled brush of the clearcut—maybe a deer, possibly a bear. We have already cleaned our plates and pans, and put the food back into the car parked up at the logging road that brought us here. We sit by the fire talking quietly of things that seem appropriate and natural to this occasion. Sometimes we put tobacco prayers into the fire, or meditate on the patterns and subtle colors of the flames. Like the quester, we too are calming the mind and coming into full presence with the wilderness, and our reason for being here.

Next morning the birds awaken me before dawn. I cherish the coziness of my sleeping bag for a few minutes, reviewing my dreams, then unzip my way out of bag and tent. The clouds are dense, muffling the world, and droplets hang on every leaf and needle. I stir the fire into wakefulness, folding back the tarp covering the wood we have gathered, and select small branches for a quickly hot blaze.

My helper emerges from the tent and begins heating water for tea as I make my way over the hummocky ground to the medicine wheel for morning prayers. On this second day I begin in the South, moving the seeker's tobacco pouch from yesterday's station in the East to today's position in the South. In the cold of early morning I pray that the seeker's inner fire burn strongly, that his desire for a purposeful life find its sacred path.

The second day is often one that confronts ego. It has neither the excitement and anticipation of the first day (and its interesting tasks of reaching and setting up a quest space) nor the relief and exhaustion of the final day. The mind may be quieter now but the ego may not. It tends to speak through the body, complaining of discomfort, worrying about dangers, and conjuring visions of food.

When fasting, the second day is often the most difficult. Cravings alternate with nausea and dizziness as the body shifts its balances and functional modes. Though this shift can actually benefit the body, the ego interprets it as threatening or unwelcome. The ego mutters to the seeker about how nice some pizza would be, or even just an orange. It does not want to be spiritual. It wants a hot shower, a soft bed, someone to cuddle, dry socks, a back rub, FOOD. It cannot figure out why you wanted to come sit in the middle of nowhere for three days and starve.

Dealing with ego is a matter of purposeful priority of awareness. Compassionate acknowledgment of ego's concerns allows the seeker to move on to a larger experience of Self, nourished by the quest's immediacy of connectedness to the web of life.

As I finish the dawn round of prayers, I see a deer stepping through the mist toward the river. Above it, and the mist, a hawk unfolds from a high tree limb and wings slowly southward. I put tobacco on the wheel for these beings, and fix their appearances in my memory to tell the quester. Everything is significant—the vision quest ceremony invokes an extended sacred space into which whatever needs to be seen is drawn. Attention must stay on a level congruent with that sacred space.

I join my helper at the cheerful fire, accepting the bowl of hot cereal she offers. When supporting someone on a vision quest I think of them while I eat. I try to share the blessings of food's nourishment through the subtle plane, in the form of prayer for the quester's sustenance and in the form of gratitude for life's giveaway. I eat for that person as well as for myself. People sometimes laugh when I say this, but the food, like the camp's fire, is an element of the quester's support. The seeker's well-being is held present in thoughts and actions that keep well-being in awareness. More than once seekers have told me they could smell what I was eating, though they were miles away.

Today my helper will go off alone for some hours to meditate and pray. One of us stays in camp at all times. As morning opens its light, the mist dissipates and blue sky peers at us through thinning clouds. Pleased with the prospects, my helper packs a lunch and her poncho (just in case) and disappears into the trees.

I clean our breakfast dishes, then perch on an eight-hundred-ringed stump the size of a Volkswagen, with my rattle. A buzzard circles the far end of the clear-cut. Smaller birds rustle through briars. I hear a squirrel scolding off in the direction my helper has gone. The ground gently steams in the sunlight. I feel the spirit of the tree whose stump I sit upon.

The sun moves higher, bringing more light into the valley. I pick up the rattle, shaking it softly, softly, no imposition on the integrity of this place, only part of the morning, the rising, the moving of day. I sing—deer song, deft-footed song, part of this land and its spring flowers. Two ducks rise from the river, quick-beating wings, circle and fly upstream toward the seeker's questing place. In the forest a grouse drums.

Later, after lunch, my helper returns smiling. "Saw a little green snake," she says, "the color of the moss." She busies herself around camp while I make my forays among the trees to gather firewood. Most of it is saturated, and I pile it next to the fire to dry.

That night my helper brings out her drum and we sing beside our warm beacon. A coyote sings too, far away; another answers, closer. The moon is full, floating high in the clear night sky. Its silver is balance to our fire's gold. The air is cold, alive with spirits as though another world has been catalyzed by moonlight. It is midnight when I make a final round of prayers at the silvered wheel.

The third day and night, the West turning, is often when movement in the heart is most strong. Deep feelings emerge—anguish or exaltation, or a long-awaited equanimity that is in itself a power conducive to vision. Prayer becomes a no-frills affair, a direct expression of feelings. The mind is tired, the body is tired, the ego is tired. The fasting gives a sense of lightness and lucidity, and the boundaries between self and surroundings have worn thin. The seeker has become familiar with every stone, tree, insect, and plant in his circle, intimately knows the textures of the ground, has surrendered to the weather, has exhausted his fears. At this point, if not before, things may shift. Consciousness may find doors of nonordinary awareness or super-ordinary awareness, especially if the quester has remained wakeful in the nights and prayed with constancy. At this time the seeker may know self and Self more clearly, and hopefully more compassionately, than at any other time.

The kind weather of the second day is matched by the warmth and blue of the third. I am the one hiking off on this day as my helper maintains a presence in camp. I do not go far, only to the lone fir at the edge of the clear-cut. Each time I come here I pay respects to this sentinel, this survivor of carnage.

It is slow going across the clear-cut. The ground's machine-made unevenness is hidden by tough grasses and barbed vegetation. Stumps and crisscrossed logs create an obstacle course that easily traps an unwary ankle in too much of a hurry. I am well heated by the time I reach the tree, and our camp is out of sight in a deceptive fold of the slope.

Here the river's voice is louder, the shade of the old forest closer, and the head must tip back to view the mountaintops. I make prayers and offerings, speaking to the tree as to an elder. I rest against its trunk, feeling its life, its memories; I taste its sap, amber tear that has softened in the sunlight. In time I return across the clear-cut to find my helper preparing lunch. In the long afternoon we feed the fire, wash ourselves, and spend much time being quiet, gazing into distances, becoming part of the land. We keep track of any human movement over the logging road, or on the hiking trail that climbs above the river. This early in the year there is little traffic on either.

Clouds gather late in the day, making a dramatic sunset, and then it is night again. I pray for the seeker's safety, for his heart to be courageous through the hours of dark. I pray his dreams give vision, if the quester sleeps, and for focus to stay present as his time on the mountain comes to an end.

Off and on throughout each day and night, and especially during prayer times, I try to check in with how the quester is doing. In maintaining a sacred space, I ask for help from whatever local spirits or usual guides and guardians will lend their benevolent attentions to our purposes. I try to establish good relationship with the beings who abide in the questing area.

All this is done with respect for whatever is best for the situation in a larger sense, and to whatever will not interfere with the quester's rightful experience. The checking in is receptive rather than intrusive. It helps guide my prayers and focus of support.

When I assist people with vision-questing I always accompany them to their quest site, not only so I can find them later, if need be, but so I can orient to that place when, from a distance, I psychically check in on their state of being. If their desire for complete privacy and independence precludes this, I do not do this monitoring.

There was one time I overdid it. The seeker had chosen a cliff edge for his quest site. Hikers had gone into that part of the forest during the day and had not returned. In the dark of the second evening I had a feeling of something amiss. The seeker was an experienced woodsman, and very hardy, but I asked the Panther totem to check in on him. "Don't let him see you," I cautioned, because the seeker's perception at that point might well be sensitive enough to note the Panther's presence. "Don't intrude on his situation—just check on him."

On return, the Panther assured me that the quester was safe. "He didn't see me," the Panther said.

When I went to meet the seeker at the end of his quest he recounted what had occurred during his time on the cliff. He described how, on the second evening, he'd suddenly felt he was being watched by a mountain lion. "I was positive of it," he said. "It was back among the trees stalking me. I was terrified! I lay there planning exactly what to do when it pounced—how I'd roll off the cliff, taking it with me."

As he talked my heart sank. "Oh no!" I thought. "That wasn't what I wanted to have happen at all. Oh dear!" I confessed my part in the matter, and he had a good laugh from it, though the terror had stayed with him for some hours after he felt the presence withdraw. Since then I have been more careful with monitoring.

Rain sprinkles a few times during the third night. Each time I wake and send prayers for the seeker.

In the morning a thousand spider webs glisten across the clear-cut. My final prayers at the wheel focus on the North—on bringing vision into life's manifestation. I pray for integration of spiritual and Earthly endeavor, and for the quester's strength and beauty on his path.

After breakfast I load my daypack with a small thermos of broth, a few apples, my smudge kit, and a raincoat. While I'm gone my helper will break camp, leaving only the fire and medicine wheel. I set off at a leisurely pace toward the quester's place, wanting to give him plenty of time to finish in solitude, clear his site, and begin the walk down.

As I near the point where the trail enters the forest I see a large bird overhead below the heavy clouds. I stop. It is an eagle coming from the quester's direction. Thrilled by this auspicious presence, I make a prayer of gratitude with tobacco I have in my pocket. In the middle of doing this another eagle appears. I straighten, craning my neck as eagle after eagle passes over me following the river's course. I count twenty and then, after a pause, there is one more. They disappear in the clouds and distance like a dream. With light steps I enter the forest.

Being the first person encountered after someone's days and nights alone, fasting and praying in the wilderness, carries with it some responsibility for treating that transition gently and respectfully. It is a gift like that given midwives, of being the first to receive what comes newborn from the other worlds.

As I see the quester coming down the path I stop and wait. He smiles, brief and shy, and eases his pack to the ground when he reaches me. "Hey," I say, quiet in the quiet, "Welcome back." We embrace, lightly, then with more conviction, and he lets me smudge him. We sit on a fallen log beside the trail and I unpack water, broth, and apples, and hand him a cup of hot broth. It gives him time to adjust to my presence. He sips the nourishing liquid, sighs, stares into the cup. Slowly he begins to speak in a low voice. It is not a conversation. I listen deeply. It is a gift of trust, precious gift of this holy, intimate experience on the mountain. My heart holds it like a new-hatched bird.

The telling of the vision at that moment is done for several reasons. In the telling that is so immediate is a fixing of it, not only in memory, but in memory that has not begun to shift from what was actually felt and experienced. Contact with ordinary context causes that shift, regardless of how honest and aware the person is. This first telling, then, is the most direct expression of the true experience.

The telling also invokes feedback from the supporter that also carries immediacy of truth. The practitioner, from her linked experience with the quester, can give perspective that also emerges directly from the quest process. Great care must be exerted in giving this perspective, however, so that it does not obscure the seeker's own reality. I am very hesitant about interpreting experience for others. Much of what happens during a vision quest is meant to gradually unfold in understanding and relevancy over time, not to be neatly packaged and presented to the seeker by the practitioner. I am also wary of too much talk at this transition point in the quest. The seeker's telling is one thing, and only includes what he wants to share. A lot of back and forth discussion quickly dissipates the quester's power, and abruptly brings the situation to a mundane level of interaction.

The seeker finishes his cup of broth and shakes his head when I offer an apple. We slip our packs on, and I let him set a pace down the trail. There is an air of primal-ness about him, of the wilds, and of finding he can become part of that environment—can endure rain, cold, dark, lack of shelter, vulnerability, hunger, loneliness. There is a peace in him, and a strength; solitude is in his eyes, but also a vision of connectedness. We hike mostly in silence, pausing a few times to catch breath after climbs. I make a small joke about his prequest trepidation of spiders, pointing out the web caught in his hair. He grunts, combs his fingers through the tangle, shakes his head over the cedar twigs that come out.

We arrive at the dismantled campsite before noon. My helper loads our packs into the car while I make prayers of gratitude at the wheel and fire. The quester gazes around as if he has suddenly reached civilization. He eats an apple while we douse the fire and return the wheel's components to the land.

From here we drive to the sweat lodge, where a one-round ceremony is carried out and the pipe at last is smoked. The seeker presents me with a blanket, and arranges for his postquest feast. This will be his formal return to community and his second telling of the quest experience, shared with those supporters who prayed for him, and with his friends and loved ones.

From time to time questers get back in touch with the practitioners who help them, asking for further resource or counsel. As a practitioner I carry each quester's vision within me, giving wider reality to its truth just as does each other person who hears that vision in a sacred way, so it may be carried even beyond the quester's death. I helped a man with cancer do a vision quest less than a year before he died, and the truth he experienced lives on in each person touched by that event. The vision seeking ceremony deals not with personal destiny alone.

The maintaining of sacred space that is part of the practitioner's service in this ceremony extends into long-range honoring of each seeker's vision. This does not mean that all the details of each quest are remembered by the practitioner. It is more like the way medicine bundles are kept, wrapped and otherwise cared for in the ways appropriate to those bundles.

It takes commitment and responsibility to work with vision seekers. Because of my way of monitoring from a distance and the individual attention I feel each quester needs, I do not work with more than four seekers during any one ceremonial cycle. Some practitioners work with larger groups of questers and usually have more assistants helping them. As more people become involved, the process takes on a different feel, and perhaps orients less to traditional purposes and procedures.

The Sky is the Direction of freedom and limitless possibility. The less baggage the quester brings, the stronger his inner experience tends to be—the more he stretches into possibilities and places he would not have thought accessible. The form itself provides sufficient stability and structure. As a coming-of-age ceremony (at any point in life), it is a gateway into both spiritual freedom and spiritual maturity, the individual journey linked with awareness of larger community.

Most quest intentions I hear articulated fall into two categories, and I sometimes think it would cause less confusion and disappointment if what was enacted carried names such as these, when appropriate, instead of "vision quest." The first category is prayer-questing, a time for addressing personal or larger concerns in an earnest and deeply engaged fashion. The second category is alliance-questing—seeking powerful awareness of life's sacred web and nourishing connections within it. Sometimes both categories of intention are present in a quest. Sometimes vision occurs during the fulfillment of either one.

What many people—perhaps most people—experience through vision questing is not visionary in its traditional sense, and this is the source of confusion or disappointment. The confusion comes in labeling something a vision that is really a state of exaggerated awareness. In this state the seeker may find insight, connection, a different level of perception, or flashes of nonordinary experience. Realizations and clarity may emerge from this without there being an actual "vision."

A feeling of significance about what is usually regarded as ordinary may elicit an intensity of focus that opens the quester to messages from spirit (or that mirrors something from the quester's consciousness). There is great value in what happens in a state of heightened attention and receptivity, but it is a misnomer to call what comes from it "vision."

The disappointment some people feel at not having a "real" vision need not be so acute if it is understood and accepted that there is much to be learned and honored from all aspects of the quest experience. Regardless if a vision occurs or not, the experience can be life-changing in other important ways. For modern people, just the act of being *with* the wilderness is an opportunity for healing in the larger web of relationship.

The confusion about what constitutes visionary experience has tended modern people toward a direction that often uses vision-questing for purposes more psychological than spiritual. As with the differences between visualization and shamanic trance, I think it helps to discern what is being done in order to make the best possible use of whatever it is. Both confusion and disappointment seal the quester off from the actual, and powerful, good of his experience.

Questers who do have visionary experiences often are those with an extraordinary degree of commitment or who have a facility with nonordinary states of consciousness. I say often—not always—because the gift of vision comes for many reasons beyond what is predictable. This is one of the mysteries that gives this ceremony its endurance in human spirituality.

Truth can't be called
falconlike to the gauntleted fist.
In dreams, naked
the mind paces behind scenes
shadowless
and light comes beyond starlight
turning aside the past, shadowless.
In dreams I find the same house
over and over,
and waking, hands stone-warmed
know not who I am.
Beside the teacher's calm voice
it is I who lose patience,
who veer from the spilled cups,
who will not stand amid my thoughts.
There are long times between, sometimes,
then truth like a butterfly
alights on the open palm
or sometimes in ways more peculiar
it comes, and somewhere leads me.

PART SEVEN

Center

MYSTERY

The manifested matrix—differentiated form, energy, and consciousness—and the unmanifested matrix—the formless light of pure consciousness—emanate from the Mystery.

People have many names for the Ultimate: Great Spirit, Goddess,
God, and so on. Having no cognizant grasp of the Ultimate I do not
know what, if anything, *is* ultimate, but I call the source of awareness
Mystery. It is divine in the sense of being beyond illusion, and therefore an orientation that can lead consciousness out of the suffering of
illusion. I do not equate the Mystery with Goddess/God/Grand-
father/Deity. Concepts of these conventionally include some level of
personification that in itself diminishes or circumscribes divinity.

Personification makes something easier to think about, relate to,
and envision, or gives embodiment to its attributes. The Mystery,
however, has no identity to describe. It is always more than can be
imagined. I view Spirit as the substance by which the Mystery
engages in pure consciousness. Deity, then, is the ultimate form of
Spirit, but is not its source.

The projection of image onto deity reveals how you think about
yourself, what you were taught about the divine as a child (or rectifi-
cation of what you were taught), cultural influences, or connections
to certain archetypes. Some personification is image-making, some is
invocation of Spirit's embodiment. Personified aspects of deity can be
the focus of powerful links in consciousness, a process valuable to
human evolvement. The spiritual stories that encode wisdom about

origins and evolution, that help us to know how to live rightly, always use personification. Whether gods and goddesses or forces enrobed in nature's forms, these personifications help us understand and *feel*— because we too are embodied—those teachings and that record of experience.

It is interesting to note the bias revealed in religions such as Christianity that always personify deity in human form (usually male); the idea being that humans were made in his image, therefore he looks like a man. In contrast, some Native stories identify the Creator as Coyote, for instance—certainly a different perspective to consider. Religions older than Christianity tended to view Spirit as multiaspected.

Often, seeing deity as one particular embodiment defines the center by one peripheral expression, like limiting your experience of the medicine wheel to a single Direction. An affinity with one Direction/one aspect of deity is natural, but can inhibit full awareness. Another approach is to dualize deity into male and female forms. This too has traditional roots in some religions.

The Mystery is not confined to any form or aspected arrays. The breath moves in the body, is essential to its function, but is not the body. The Mystery moves in the breath but is not the breath. It moves in the wind, the stone, the distant star, the Spirit, but is not thereby defined. Beyond the infinite, unspoken matrix of pure Mind abides formless dimensions of consciousness, and that does not define the Mystery either.

I am not frustrated at these insufficient words. As I complete the writing of this book I am reminded again of how preposterous it is to set thoughts on paper and offer them as truths of some kind. It is only a way of participating. This book has been one turn of the wheel—a record of experience, not a destination. My prayer is that it honors love, and the beauty life has given.

The mandala explored here has spiraled to center. Looking East you see the realm of mind and its potential to initiate intention and understanding. To the South is the gift of evolution through interdependency and encounter. Turning West you find the teachings of the mature heart, and the fluidity to continue growing and changing.

Looking North you see the possibilities of manifested spirit, the opportunity to embody well-being.

Beneath is the Earth, the experience of nourishment in a community of life, the orientation to cycles of unfoldment. Above is the Sky, the reaching into destiny, the vision of what can be, the desire to know. The matrices are experienced in all these realms, concentric ripples extending in all Directions, a sphere without boundary. Awareness can spiral inward to center, self becoming Self becoming more. One journey echoes the other until the notion of path loses delineation. Your world can dissolve and be remade in consciousness each moment.

The sense of losing control is a liberation of capacity to accept ever-increasing ranges of reality, loosening illusion's hold. I do not know if this is true for other sorts of spiritual practitioners, but the paths of shamanic adepts seem to originate from a basic destabilization in consciousness. The destabilization gives an experience of reality that defies conventional perspectives. Shamans-to-be are either born with this or with a propensity that is, at some point, catalyzed.

When I meet people who want shamanic training I look for this destabilization, but its presence is not all that is needed. There has to be a reference core providing useful orientation, guidance, and discernment; there has to be a capacity for discipline, courage, and ethical behavior. These are things that make destabilization something besides a potential for madness. People lacking that inherent destabilization can simulate it or situationally replicate it, but the ones who do this still move differently within consciousness. It is like someone born blind and someone who, on occasion, wears a blindfold (or who loses sight as an adult). The latter still remembers how things looked through the eyes, and is influenced by that basis.

What natural shamans usually develop is not perception but control: how to shift attention away from, or filter, nonordinary awareness; how to keep the mind aligned; how to deal with isolation and fear; how to maintain. What is often not learned is how to participate in society, how to share experience, and how to and when to let go of control.

The control, a survival tool, can easily become a barrier—a mechanism of fear. Control strategies applied to the inner reality echo in approaches used in external situations and relationships. Loss of inner control is associated with madness; loss of outer control threatens cohesiveness of relationships. Both of these stem from fear of isolation or fragmentation. In our society, conventional reality is presented as the haven of sanity, acceptance, mutual experience, beliefs, knowledge, and safety. A person whose consciousness is not stabilized within that reality (illusory as it may be) is, in our society, outcast. Some people embrace this position and find place for their particular skills or see it in more positive terms. Some people simply go mad. And there is a wide spectrum of other responses between these poles.

One way to relax control and address fear is to realize a less loaded perspective of reality. To view conventional reality as either an illusion or as an elusive standard of sanity is to place it in opposition to whatever your nonordinary reality is. Certainly conventional reality is illusory. But so is your nonordinary reality, ultimately. It is just that ordinary reality is a more widely shared model.

There are truths within conventional reality. They are not ultimate truths; they are verifiable truths operable in a particular system of perception and experience, and as such are valuable. These truths include ethics, and principles of right action, honorable endeavor, and compassionate perspective. There are truths in conventional reality's physics and mathematics, truths in its arts, and so on.

This is likewise for nonordinary realities. Within each is a strata of experience from which verifiable truths can be derived. I use "verifiable" in the Buddhist sense that distinguishes confused perception (or sheer delusion) from what has actual cause and effect within a particular reality (though the reality be ultimately illusory).

Imagine you are watching a play. The actor places a necklace around the actress's throat. The person beside you, who has poor vision, mutters, "He's strangling her." The verifiable truth is that the actor is putting a piece of jewelry around the woman's neck; the perception of strangling is confused, but both are applied to an illusion of reality—that being the play.

If purposefulness is understood and commitment clear, a participation in either conventional or nonordinary reality becomes an investment in spiritual evolution. This honors the opportunities present in whatever context your consciousness perceives, without grasping at any of them as a reference for sanity or ultimate identity.

This gives the disciplines of control a more utilitarian function, shifting them away from being reflexes of fear. A simple but powerful thing to remember when consciousness seems too far "out there" is that you do not have to be there, and if you accept being there, you do not have to be afraid. You are neither crazy nor lost, and your reality is no more or less true than any other. What is reliable is movement—you can align awareness and continue the journey home.

Your alignment to Spirit leads you back, again and again, as you integrate experience, understanding, and core beliefs in what you find most good. It is your nature to be an expression of that good; it is your natural spirituality.

One autumn I was visiting a city in the midwest, doing some teaching. The people I stayed with asked for a sweat ceremony, so we built a lodge at a private retreat center several hours out of the city. We planned to sweat the next evening, but that day it rained continuously—a cold autumn downpour. We loaded the van anyway, and drove toward the retreat center as evening darkened an already gray day. The rain steadily washed down, but we decided to sweat regardless of weather.

It did not let up as we made our way down the slippery dirt road leading to the retreat center, but in the instant of turning into the driveway the rain completely ceased as though we had crossed into another world. Not another drop fell all evening.

There is power in simply giving yourself to what you find most good. It does not mean that outcomes will always seem serendipitous—it is not a reward system, but something more engaging. It calls for a yielding to center, the salmon's journey home. It opens you to the particular current that washes away what holds you back. The current is the vitality by which you persevere. In giving yourself to that journey, you make fuller contact with life and its potentials.

There are great challenges in the current, but also those times when the rain stops like magic, when the eagle dips its wings to you on the mountaintop, when the light of Spirit comes into silence with a song forged in truth.

Blessings to you, and gratitude for your listening.

Appendix

WHEEL PERSPECTIVES

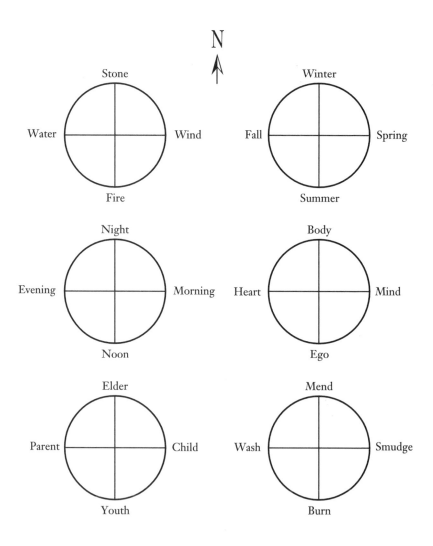

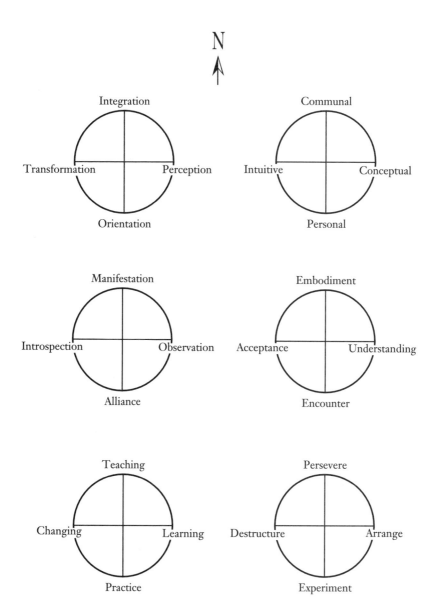

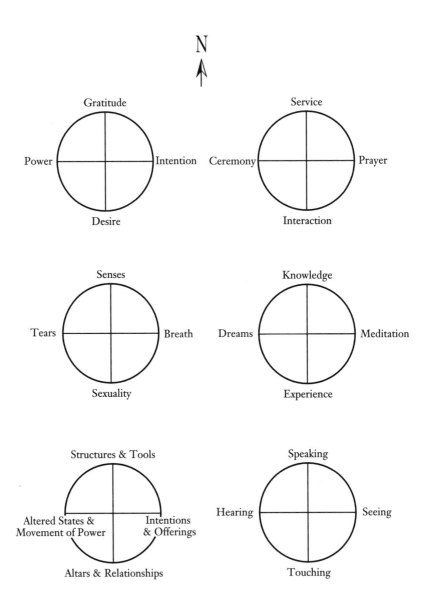

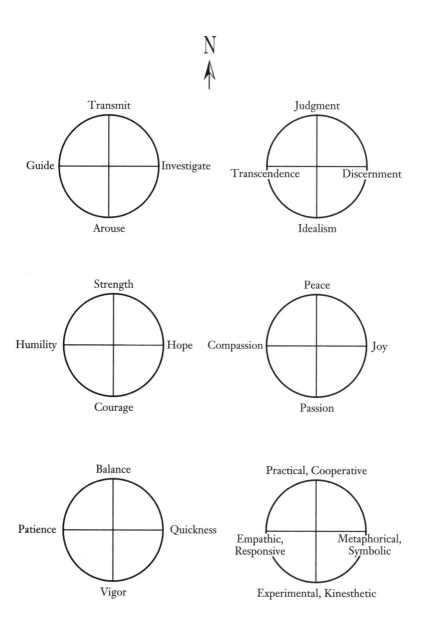

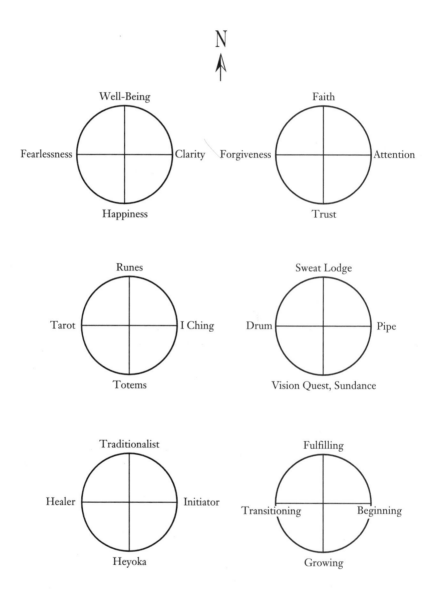

N

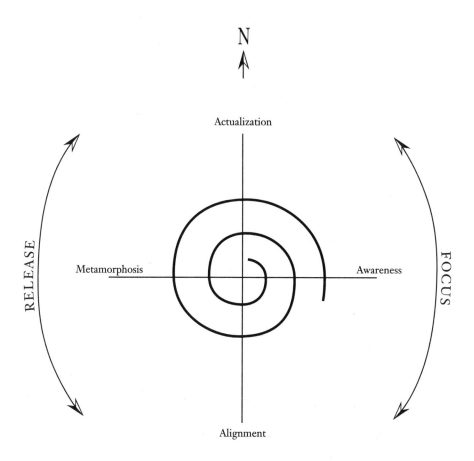

Actualization

Metamorphosis

Awareness

Alignment

RELEASE

FOCUS

The Spirit of Place
A Workbook for Sacred Alignment
Loren Cruden • ISBN 0-89281-511-6 • $16.95 pb

Arranged to follow the progress of the seasons, *The Spirit of Place* offers ideas and ceremonies for developing a spirituality that is indigenous to the land and accessible to everyone. Visualizations and prayers focus the mind; acknowledging totems and allies strengthens the will; meditation centers the spirit; and heightened intuition opens the heart to change and acceptance. Essential companions in these practices are the plants, animals, and minerals sharing our world. Useful for people at all levels of experience, *The Spirit of Place* can be returned to again and again, to challenge and inspire. Its wisdom leads us to a greater spiritual attunement with the cycles of our living Earth.

Coyote s Council Fire
Contemporary Shamans on Race, Gender, and Community
Loren Cruden • ISBN 0-89281-566-3 • $14.95 pb

Shamanism is a spiritual path that emphasizes close connections with the environment, and as environments change, so too must shamanism change. But how can one distinguish between healthy innovation and degenerate corruptions of tradition? Drawing on decades on involvement in the shamanic community, Loren Cruden offers her perspective on these often heated issues, and provides a forum for a number of Native American and non-Native shamans to share their views on the subject.

Sacred Earth
The Spiritual Landscape of Native America
Arthur Versluis • ISBN 0-89281-352-0 • $10.95 pb

"Versluis offers a much-needed understanding of Native American religion. Through discussion of how the religions of Native Americans compare to traditional religions, he finds ground for a common spirituality. While contemporary society emphasizes ecology, Versluis points out that Native Americans always had a love and respect for the environment and a recognition of the spiritual qualities of nature. This book is necessary reading for those seeking a greater understanding of Native American spirituality." **Library Journal**

Navajo and Tibetan Sacred Wisdom

The Circle of the Spirit

Peter Gold • 0-89281-411-X • $29.95 pb
175 color and black-and-white illustrations

The similarity between Navajos and Tibetans has often been noted by scholars: the mandala sand paintings common to both cultures, their profound ideas about matter and spirit, as well as the uncanny physical resemblance between the two peoples. In *Navajo and Tibetan Sacred Wisdom*, anthropologist Peter Gold draws extensive parallels between the two cultures' creation myths, cosmology, geomancy, psychology, visionary arts, and healing and initiation rituals.

"A bold and exciting exploration, showing many astonishing parallels between these precious and imperiled traditions, from which our own world-weary western culture has so much to learn." **Peter Matthiessen**
Author of The Snow Leopard *and* Indian Country

Island of the Sun

Mastering the Inca Medicine Wheel

Alberto Villoldo and Erik Jendresen • ISBN 0-89281-520-5 • $14.95 pb

Island of the Sun recounts Alberto Villoldo's return to Peru in search of the Quechua Indian shaman Don Jicaram, first encountered in *Dance of the Four Winds*, who had initiated him into the secrets of the Inca Medicine Wheel and the spiritual journey of the Four Winds.

"Profound and personal, cosmic and compassionate…memoir, Andean adventure, and quest for wisdom, the book is an even deeper, wiser, more moving tour of the extraordinary, with Villoldo a refreshing guide, frank and engaging."
San Francisco Chronicle

"A narrative rich in myth, history, and metaphor." Booklist

These and other Inner Traditions titles are available at many bookstores or, to order directly from the publisher, send a check or money order for the total amount, payable to Inner Traditions, plus $3.00 shipping and handling for the first book and $1.00 for each additional book to:

Inner Traditions, P.O. Box 388, Rochester, VT 05767